70 Objections and How to overcome Them

Contents

Introduction

What is Business Development? Business development is a term that refers to the process of developing and improving your business. This includes things like increasing revenue, expanding into new markets, or making sales in your developing business. Business development can be done through various methods including:
- Sales
- Marketing campaigns
- Public relations strategies
- Business intelligence

This book will focus on one particular aspect of Business Development: how to make sales in your company's developing industry by overcoming objections from potential customers.

A business development manager's job is not an easy one. They are tasked with the responsibility of making sales in their developing business, and overcoming objections to these sales.

It's important to be able to make sales in your developing business. Business Development is key and you need to do what it takes to get people interested in what you're selling.

The road to success in business is not always a straight one. Business owners often face objections from their customers, and these can come in all shapes and sizes.

"70 Objections And How To Overcome Them" is a step-by-step guide on how to make sales in your developing business. Businesses often face objections before they can close the sale, and it's important to know how to overcome these obstacles or deal with them appropriately. This book goes through every objection that you might come across and offers you solutions for dealing with them.

Businesses in today's world need a way to deal with these issues so they can make the most out of every sale opportunity!

Essential Elements of the Sales Cycle

In the simplest of terms, a sales cycle refers to a series of events that you go through with a customer, from the initial introduction to the close and follow-through. There are short sales cycles and long sales cycles, depending on (among other things) the type of product you're selling, the cost of the item, and who your customers are. There are innumerable variations on sales cycles, but they all have several elements in common.

The important thing to remember is that with every element of the sales cycle that is done correctly and effectively, you reduce the number of objections you're going to get by a wide margin. Objections arise when you're selling to the wrong market, when you're not asking the right questions, and when you're making presentations that aren't geared to-ward customers' needs. When you haven't met the standards that each of these steps requires, you'll never get beyond the objections to reach the close.

Following are the five most common elements of the sales cycle.

Prospecting

Prospecting is the art of looking for customers in all the right places. Suppose you pick the wrong people to call on, you're going to have a much more difficult time selling your product. It's like a manager who hires the wrong person. No amount of training, coaching, and motivating will help mold someone who is not right for the job into the company's best employee.

How your prospect depends, once again, on what it is you're selling, whether your company gives you sales leads and a territory to mine or whether you're the one who deter-mines where to look for customers. One of the products I market is geared toward children, so I want to sell to companies who sell to kids. One way I prospect is to go to stores that sell children's products, go to the racks, and check out the product packaging. When I find a product that I think is in a similar category to mine, I look on the back of the pack-age and find the address, phone number, and Website of the company. Because these are companies that already have real estate in these stores, they are logical prospects to go after to see if they will carry my product.

Often, prospecting is seen as a numbers game—the more prospects you have, the greater your chances of making a sale. That is true, and the most successful salespeople, no matter what they're selling, live, sleep, and eat prospecting. But they also know that it's the □uality of the time they spend prospecting that makes the difference; it's not just the numbers that count, it's how they can show □ualified prospects the added value they bring. Here are four ways they do it:

1. Cultivate the gatekeepers. In one of the sections on appointment objections, we talked about getting past the gatekeeper. But sometimes the best way to storm the gate is to make friends with the gatekeeper. The decision-maker's assistant or secretary can be your greatest ally; he or she often has more influence than we give credit for. When an assistant has been helpful to me, I'll call the receptionist and get his or her

full name and the address. Then I send a card that says, "Time. Your most valuable commodity" on the front, and on the inside, "Thanks for sharing some of it with me." I hand write a line or two inside, insert my business card, and mail it off immediately. It's excellent, the difference that small step makes the next time I call.

2. Call potential prospects during off hours. The worst time to try and reach decision-makers are during the day, when he or she is on the phone or running to meetings. Instead, call at 7:30 or 8 a.m., before everyone gets there, or at 5:30 or 6:00 when everyone's left. Call the Friday before holiday week-ends when most people are in a good mood and the office is emptying out. Try Saturday mornings. Many high level executives go into the office when it's □uiet, and they can get paperwork done. They'll be more likely to speak to you if you're the only one calling. It also shows them that you're working as hard as they are, and will likely continue to do so after you sell them something.

3. Cultivate creativity. One of the most successful real estate agents I ever met got most of her business through a gas station. She made friends with the attendant at the station she patronized and gave him her business card. This station was the first one off the highway into an area where many new homes were being built. She asked the attendant to give her card to anyone who stopped to ask for directions or ask about a Realtor. She made many new contacts this way. Remember this saying that I once found in a for-tune cookie: Those who have a thing to sell and go and whisper in a well, aren't so apt to get the dollars as one who climbs a tree and hollers.
4. Be tenacious. Keep trying new ways to get the ac-count. Send prospects new and updated information that might assist them in making their decision. Keep sending notes, faxing, and e-mailing ideas of value to them. Or send them a chocolate sneaker with a card that says, "Now that I got one foot in the door, I'd like to find ways we can help your organization with our products and services." When the time comes to buy, it is your name—and your tenacity — they will remember.

Great salespeople have many traits in common. They ask smart □uestions, know how to close, and have excellent follow-through. But the one trait they demonstrate more consistently than any other is constant prospecting, enhanced by creative approaches that build value and relationships.

To put it in other words, great salespeople see opportunity everywhere—and they make the calls. They know it's not just the numbers, but the numbers are what count.

Qualifying

Every □uestion you ask is a qualifying question. There are, of course, basic □uestions that uncover needs, time frame, budget, and decision-makers. But all your □uestions should be designed to help you determine if your product or service is right for this prospect (and that's what □ualifying is all about, isn't it?).

Qualifying □uestions help you understand the uniqueness of each prospect. Take notes so that you can document key points and pick up what's most important to a prospect. Closing is not difficult when it is a natural extension of your relationship with a prospect, based upon your understanding of the benefits your product or service can provide him.

Asking, the right questions is essential to making sure your product, is a good match with each prospective customer. In other words, you've got to □ualify that the person you're speaking to has a need for your product or service, has the money, and has the authority to buy. Otherwise, you end up wasting much time—yours and the customer's.

Many beginning salespeople end up going back to a potential customer several times because they don't under-stand which product the customer wants or needs. They have just one qualifying □uestion: "Before we get started, if I could show you something that could benefit you and your business, do we have a basis for doing business today?" And they fully expect the prospect to say yes. What could he possibly object to in that □uestion? But they don't really know where to go from there.

They have no idea what would benefit that prospect; consequently, they have no way to move the sale forward. Experience teaches that you have to ask questions to pin-point each customer's needs and desires. If you don't ⬚ualify customers properly, you not only waste a lot of time, you ultimately hurt your reputation, and your company's as well.

Presentation

Sales calls come in as many different shapes and sizes as there are products to sell. Some sales calls are just ex-tended conversations, where both seller and buyer profit from the end result. For most salespeople, however, there comes a time when a more formal sales presentation is necessary to close the deal. Here are five steps you can take in any situation to make your presentations powerful and persuasive:

1. **Prepare**, prepare, prepare. Before you make any presentation, you must complete a thorough needs analysis so that you uncover the prospect's hot but-tons and address the prospect's needs. Make notes of the most important things you want to cover (don't, however, read from your notes directly— people get a much stronger message when it is spoken from the heart instead of the page). Do as much research as possible. Peter Conneley, currently President and CEO of Global Advertising and Marketing for www.tommy.com (a division of Tommy Hilfiger), says salespeople who come un-prepared have no chance of doing business with him. "Sometimes people will come in with a presentation," he says, "and tell me they have a great idea for my company. But when I ask if they've seen any of our new stores, they say no. And when I ask if they've seen our new ad campaign, they say no. If I were going to meet the head of marketing for a corporation, I would certainly review the ad campaign. If they haven't, that's the end of their presentations."

2. **Follow the four Ts.** Don't launch into your solutions immediately. Start with a short introduction. Build rapport with the

people in the room. Make sure everyone is comfortable, and that you know how much time you have. Then follow the four Ts of presentations:

- Tell them what you're going to tell them. Let them know what to expect in the presentation, and why your solution makes sense. For instance, you might say, "I'm now going to take you through our new product line and demonstrate exactly how it will help you decrease production time."

- Tell them. Go through your presentation following the outline you just proposed.

- Test them. Keep your prospect involved. Don't just spit out information; ask □uestions that will let you know if the presentation is hitting home and addressing his criteria. Ask, "Is that important to you?" Or "Do you see how this could help eliminate the service problem you had in the past?"

- Tell them what you told them. Summarize your ideas and the most important benefits you covered in your presentation. Leave the prospect with the knowledge that you have hit on the points that are most important to him.

3. **Be yourself**. Don't worry about making your presentation perfect; concentrate on making your con-tent strong and powerful. Speak as if you were having an informal one-to-one conversation, no matter how many people you're actually addressing. Once you've done your preparation and know the four Ts, you can relax and let your personality come through.

4. **Present** with passion and pizzazz. You don't have to be an entertainer or magician, but you do need enthusiasm and a positive attitude. A study conducted by Harvard Business School determined that four factors are critical to success in business:

information, intelligence, skill, and attitude. When these factors were ranked in importance, this particular study found that information, intelligence and skill, combined, amounted to seven percent of business success, and attitude amounted to 93 per cent! If you're not enthusiastic about your presentation, it doesn't matter how much you prepare or how many hot but-tons you hit; you will lose your audience before you get anywhere near the close.

5. **Remember** that technology is just a tool. There's an old saying that goes, "If you can't convince them, confuse them." Some salespeople, intentionally or not, get so caught up in fancy graphic displays and overloaded slides, they forget about getting their core message across. Suppose you need to use graphics and handouts, fine. Just don't let your audience miss your message because they're overwhelmed with techno-logically perfect, but meaningless, information.
Franklin Delano Roosevelt may have had the best advice ever for anyone giving a presentation: "Be brief. Be sincere. Be seated." Keep your presentation short, strong, and focused. Speak from the heart, get your message across— and be seated.

Closing

I've been in the business of sales my whole life. Every single day, I'm either selling something myself or training others to be better salespeople. I have studied every closing techni☐ue ever put forward. Not only that, I've interviewed thousands of the top sales reps in the country, and they've also studied every closing techni☐ue, and come to the same conclusion. The bottom line is if you can't simply say to your customer, "Why don't we go ahead with this," there's some-thing wrong. Not with your closing, but with your approach to sales.
The truth is that no one has yet discovered a closing technique that works unless it is built on a strong foundation.

11

If you want to know what the best closing techniques are, ask your customers. They'll tell you things such as: "The best sales reps come in here and know my business. They know who I sell to, they know what I need. They don't approach me with some generic presentation they learned by rote. They make me feel like I'm their first and best customer."

Every day you have to live with a sense of urgency: "I have a lot on my plate; how can I move things forward to-day?" But closing only has weight when it's backed by the steps you take before you ask for the order:

1. Rapport. If a customer doesn't like you, doesn't trust you, and doesn't feel comfortable with you, then it doesn't matter what closing techni□ue you use.

You don't have to be friends with all your customers, but you do have to establish some kind of bond. And how do you do that? First, by getting to know that person, understanding his or her business, and discovering how your product or service can be of benefit. The second and most important method of establishing rapport is achieved by following the best advice ever given: Be yourself. It's the only way I know to make a meaningful connection with another person. If that connection doesn't happen (and there will be instances when it doesn't), then you may be better off not doing business with that individual.

2. Relationships. The objective of establishing rapport is to form a relationship. Some relationships are built □uickly; others take time to blossom. Some are purely on a professional level, others are more personal. Part of building a relationship is being able to adapt to each customer's personality. I recently had a meeting with a potential customer in which we didn't even talk business for the first half hour. We chatted about his hobbies and interests. He needed that time to make a connection with me. Then we were able to proceed with the sale, and I closed by asking, "Why don't we go ahead with this?" Of course, along the way, I asked simple □uestions like "Wouldn't you agree?" To get

12

a series of "yes" responses. These small agreements or trial closes, test the buyer and build towards the sale. Relationships may take minutes to form, or they may take months; either way, it's the key to get-ting new customers and keeping old ones on board.

3. Needs analysis. I remember a story I once heard about a guest on The Tonight Show when Johnny Carson was the host. The guest was billed as the greatest salesman who ever lived. Johnny started off by saying, "You're the greatest salesman in the world—sell me something." Johnny expected his guest to go into a razzmatazz sales spiel. Instead, the man said, "What would like me to sell you?" "I don't know," Johnny replied. "How about this ashtray?" "Why, Johnny?" Asked the guest. "What is it that you like about that ashtray?" Carson began to list the things he liked: the fact that it matched the brown colour of his desk, that it was octagonal in shape, that it fulfilled the need for someplace to put his ashes.

Then the guest asked, "So Johnny, How much would you be willing to spend for a brown octagonal ash-tray like that one?" "I don't know," said Johnny. "Maybe $20." "Sold!" Said the greatest salesman.

The sales concept behind this interchange is under-standing what the customer needs. The secret lies in persuading the customer to state his own needs and then getting him to sell himself. After that, closing becomes a natural progression.

4. Asking for the order. You would think this would be obvious, wouldn't you? It's amazing, though, how many salespeople miss the close because they don't even ask. Usually, they're reluctant to ask because they're afraid the customer will say no. But guess what? You hardly ever get a flat no. What you get is an objection. And when you get an objection, you get the opportunity to ask uestions, find out the reason for the objection, change what you're doing, and present your solution in a better way. Then,

when you've heard the objection and discovered the solution, you can simply say, "Why don't we go ahead with this?"

The first close I ever tried was, "Would you like to put 15 per cent down on that, or is 10 per cent easier?" The funny thing is, it worked, because without even realizing it, I had established rapport, formed a relationship, discovered the customer's needs, and asked for the order. And I guarantee you, even if I just said, "Why don't we just go ahead with this," it probably would have worked too. Because it doesn't matter if you use the Ben Franklin, alternative choice, right angle, left hook close—if you can't just outright say, "let's go ahead with this," then you better examine all the skills we discussed to earn the right to close in the first place. If you don't build the foundation, the sale is being built on sand and it won't stand.

Follow-Through

According to the definition in Webster's New World Dictionary, Second Edition, the term follow-through means "the act of continuing an undertaking to completion, to its natural end." But just what is considered the "natural end" of a sale? Is it when the sale is closed? Not if you're looking for repeat business. For most people, selling requires constant cultivation; in order to keep the relationships growing you've got to look at each one and ask yourself, "What other related actions can I take today to strengthen this connection and move it towards a natural end (or at least the next natural level)?"
Most people think that follow-through is a system to ensure that everything gets done — that's only part of it. Follow-through is what you do to ensure that you build the strongest, longest-lasting relationships possible. Your enthusiasm and determination to succeed — attached to benefits for your customers — are the fuel that help you take the most effective steps to follow up and follow through.
After the close of every sale you should be asking your-self, "What can I realistically do to move this sale and this relationship

to the next level?" You can — and should — take the standard follow-up steps: When you attend a meeting, follow it up with a letter summarizing the main points of your discussion; send thank-you notes for appointments, demonstrations, orders, and referrals; send articles of personal and professional interest; and find new ways to connect with your customers.

But these steps should not be taken blindly. They must be taken while considering the benefits. Effective follow-through is not just providing additional information; it's discovering steps that you can take to increase or enhance your customer's growth and how you can help build his business beyond this particular sale.

A robot can perform standard follow-up tasks. Effective follow-up means finding out what you can bring to this relationship that someone else might not have. Think about who your customer is, what he needs most, and how you can best meet that need. Then your follow-through will come naturally. You'll be following his agenda—not yours—and providing a valuable benefit.

The Sales Cycle Checklist

Recently, somebody asked me about my early sales experiences. When I thought about being new to sales, I re-membered one company that gave me a laminated card with ☐uestions printed front and back. These questions served as a constant reminder of what I needed to do before, during, and after the sale.
Although I no longer carry this card around, it was a great tool to help me learn the business of sales and served as great reminder over the years. We all need reminders now and then, no matter how skilled we are. So here is a list of ☐uestions, similar to the ones printed on that card years ago, that can take you through the sales cycle, step-by-step.
  • When prospecting, did I:

Find the best possible resources for locating new customers?

Cultivate the gatekeeper whenever possible?
Start early and stay late—calling potential customers during off hours?

Find creative ways to find new prospects?
Stay persistent and tenacious in trying to make contact with hard-to-see executives?

When qualifying, did I:
Ask, "Is there anybody, besides yourself, who might be involved in the decision-making process?"
Ask, "What does a vendor need to do to earn your business?"
Find out how and why the decision was made to purchase the present product or service?
Find out what the time frame is?
Find out if funds have been allocated? Uncover the specific needs?
Ask all relevant ualifying uestions?
Have them go into depth by using phrases such as: "tell me about...," "describe...," and "elaborate..."?
During the presentation/demonstration, did I:
Prepare thoroughly? Follow the four Ts?
Link the presentation to the prospect's key needs? Speak from the heart and not from a script?
Present with passion and pizzazz?
Concentrate on getting my message across rather than relying too much on technology?

- When closing, did I:

Earn the right to close by following all previous steps in the sales cycle?
Build rapport?

Form a relationship?

Do a thorough needs analysis? Ask for the order?

For follow-through, did I:

Send a thank you letter for the appointment, presentation, order, and so on?

Send a summary memo?

Establish an ongoing relationship?

Discover what unique value I can bring to the table to meet this customer's ongoing needs?

No one should be asking these questions by rote. It's not a script that could or should be followed for every sale, but it is a great structure to keep in mind. Take a hint from a popular infomercial I'm sure you've seen—the one where the famous pitch man Ron Popeil tells you to "set it… and forget it." Learn this step-by-step procedure—and then forget it. Pull it out when you're puzzled by why you didn't make a sale. Maybe there's something you forgot to do that you should have remembered!

Time, experience, credentials and need

If it weren't for objections, there would be no need for salespeople at all. You could just send out a brochure that listed all the features of a product, how much it cost, and that would be that. A customer would either buy from that brochure, or find another one that he liked better.
Luckily, for those of us who love sales, the world doesn't work that way. People will always have objections. And when you get right down to it, there are only two basic questions that people are always asking (no matter what they actually say): "What is this product or service going to do for me?" And "Why should I buy it from you?"

Those ⬚uestions come out in various forms, including objections about: Time. Experience. Credentials. Need.

The reason i've put all this different types of objections into one part is because there's not often that much difference between how you handle different objections. So what you say varies, of course, according to the issue you're addressing, but the concepts behind how you handle each of these objections remain the same.

The objections I've included here are some of the most common ones salespeople across the United States tell me they hear every day. Use the objections and replies i've included here as examples, not as scripts. Adapt them to your product or service, your company, your industry, and most of all, to your individual style and personality.

Time Objections

Why do time objections arise? It's simple: People are busy. They want to get off the phone, end the meeting, or get back to the work they see as a more important way to spend their time. If you're making a sales call, especially if it's a cold call on the phone, you have no idea what's going on at the other end of the line. It could be that the customer is over-whelmed with work, or is on a tight deadline and truly does not have time to talk. Or it could be a stalling tactic, just to get you off the phone for the moment. The key is to explain why the time they invest in speaking with you is worthwhile, because it will either save them time in the long run or make them money down the line.

There are several ways to handle time objections:

Objection example:
"I don't have time to speak with you right now."

Reply Option 1:

The simplest, and sometimes best reply to that is often, "I can appreciate that your time is valuable. When would be a good time for me to call again?"

Reply Option 2:
"That's exactly why I'm calling you. Our pro-gram actually helps people save time, and I'd like to see if we can do the same for you...."

Reply Option 3:
"I understand that you're busy right now. Can you just answer one ☐uestion for me now? What is the greatest challenge facing you and your company right now? Once you tell me the answer, I'll take some time to think about ways that my product can help you meet that challenge and call you back next week. Is Wednesday after-noon good for you? Or would Thursday morning be better?"

Objection example:

"It's not the right time."

Reply:
"I can appreciate that. A lot of my customers felt the same way. But when they saw the advantages that we provided them, they said it was the best time to see me. I'd like to see if we can do the same for you."

People say that timing is everything—but it's not the only thing. If the customer can't speak with you today, or even in the near future, that's no reason to give up. Ask if it would be all right to stay in touch. Learn as much as you can about the customer, and then send information that can gradually educate him on how he can benefit from your product or service.

Objection example:
"We need it sooner."

Reply Option 1:
"How soon do you need it? And how important is it that you get it by that date?" (You want to find out if this is a real objection or if this is just a stall. You don't want to run around in circles trying to get an early delivery date if a later one will do.)

Reply Option 2:
"Let me go back and check with my production department and see if we can have it to you by that date. I don't want to make a promise to you I wouldn't be able to keep—we don't do that with our customers." (You may lose out on this particular sale if you can't make the delivery date, but the customer will appreciate your honesty and probably buy from you in the future.)

Experience Objections

Why do experience objections arise? If customers have purchased products or service from you or company in the past, and they were satisfied, they'd probably want to buy from you again. Of course, the opposite is true as well. If they have had bad experiences with your products or company— or know someone else who had a bad experience—you'll have to work a lot harder to overcome their objections. You have to let them know how things have changed for the better—
What you are doing now that was not done before, how your technology has changed, how your company has been restructured—in other words, whatever will assure them they will have a better experience this time than they had before.

Objection example:
"We used your product or service before and we didn't like it."

Reply:
"Can you explain to me exactly what it was you didn't like about our product?" (Go back to the fundamentals of the six-step method and have them define the objection for you. Perhaps the problem they had with your product has been fixed in a later

version. Perhaps they were not using it correctly. So Once you know exactly what it was they didn't like, you can explain how things are different now.)

Objection example:
"We know others who have used your product or service before and they didn't like it."

Reply:
"Do you know exactly what it was they didn't like about our product?" (This is practically the same as the previous objection. The customers may not be able to be as specific about the problem, but you can get the general idea.)
Objection example:
"We used a similar product, or service before and we didn't like it."

Reply:
"Can you explain to me exactly what it was you didn't like about that product?" (This should be an easier objection to handle because once you know what the problem was, you can point out the differences between your product or service and the one they used before.)

Testimonials: The Power of a Second Opinion

When you come across experience objections (or credential objections such as the ones in the next section), the best way to handle them is to bring in a testimonial from one of your customers. Have you ever watched one of the home shopping networks on television or seen an infomercial? Then you know about the power of testimonials. I know, from my own experience selling products on QVC, that as soon as there's a phone call from a satisfied customer, there's an instantaneous increase in the number of sales. When real customers are seen or heard testifying as to how beneficial this product has been for them, potential customers are more likely to buy. It helps the prospect clearly imagine him- or herself already the proud owner of that product, experiencing the same benefits as the customer who made the testimonial.

The best way to get prospective clients to buy from you is to introduce them to other satisfied customers. Because it's not very practical to drag satisfied customers around with you on all your sales calls, and testimonials can take their place. Luckily, you don't have to be on a shop-ping network or infomercial to use testimonials to your advantage.

Ask your best customers if you can "interview" them about the positive experiences they've had with your product and company, and record it on a video or digital camera. You can then load the videos onto your laptop computer, and play them back for prospective customers with just the click of a mouse.

For example, there are some instances when customers say that they know of others who have used your product or service and didn't like it. You can counter that statement by saying, "I understand that's what you heard from Mr Jones. But I'd like to let you see for yourself what Mr Smith had to say after he tried someone else's product, and then came to us for his next purchase."

This is the perfect customer to give you a testimonial. Then you can say to your reluctant prospects, "Here are some comments from a customer who had the same concerns as you do now. She chose competitor's product, but then came to us because of our higher ☐uality and service. Here's what she had to say." You can then open your laptop and play the testimonial for your prospect immediately.

Ask your customers to talk about the benefits they've received from using your product or service. If you have many different testimonials, you can use the one that fits best into the sales scenario in which you find yourself. One rep I know takes pictures of customers using his product. A picture of a happy, satisfied customer is worth a thousand impersonal sales brochures. You can't get closer to the truth than when it comes from someone who has real life experience with you, your product, and your company.

Credential Objections

Why do credential objections arise? This type of objection only comes up when a customer is not familiar with you, your product, and/or your company. Let's face it, here you are, a stranger, trying to get this customer to put his trust in you and to part with his hard-earned money for something with which he is completely unfamiliar! That's a tall order. It's no wonder that the customer has doubts. This may be a time, depending on what it is you're selling, when a free sample or trial period is in order, or a 30-day money-back guarantee. The idea is that once you get the customer to give your product or service a try, she'll like it so much she'll want to come back for more.
Objection example:
"i've never heard of your product or service before," or, "I've never heard of your company before."

Reply:
"I can appreciate that. We are new on the market. Some of our other customers had the same concerns. But after using our product, they found that what we had to offer was even more beneficial than the better-known product they had used in the past. So I'd like to show you how we can do the same for you. (This is a perfect time to let your customer know what makes your product different from similar products out on the market. It's also the perfect time to use a testimonial from a satisfied customer.)

Objection example:
"We've heard negative things about your product (or service)."

Reply:
"Can I ask what it was you heard and who you heard it from?" (Once again, you want to get the customer to define the objection as specifically as possible. It may be that your

competition is putting you down, or there may be a bad buzz going around the industry that you want to be aware of. You need to do a little digging so that you can provide the customer with the information he needs to make his own decision about your product or service.)

Need Objections

Why do need objections arise? In theory, a need objection will never come up because you've □ualified your prospects so carefully. In reality, need objections come up during the □ualification process. It's while you're introducing your-self, who you are, and what your product is about, that a customer will interrupt and say, "I don't need that," or "I already have someone who does that for us." These are the times when you have to stop and answer those objections before you move any farther ahead with sale.

Objection example:
"I have no need for your product (or service)."

Reply:
"I can understand where you're coming from, but maybe you can answer a few questions for me. I visited your Website and went to your downtown store, and I think that my service can help you out. Can you tell me a little bit about your goals and challenges so I can be sure my service really does fit your needs?" (By saying that you visited the Website and/or the store, you let the customer know that you've done your homework, and that you've already thought about ways you can be of benefit to him. The customer will probably be impressed that you already know so much about his business.)

Objection example:
"We don't use outside vendors."

Reply:

You would start off by asking, "Why is that?" The customer might reply with something such as, "We've used them in the past and found they weren't as effective as our own internal resources." You would follow that by asking, "Can you expand on the problem you had in the past?" You want to get as much knowledge as you can about what caused them to stop using outside vendors. Then you can go back the Feel, Felt, Found scenario: "I had a customer you're welcome to talk to who felt the same way. But after she gave our service a try, she found that what we did was far be-yond what she had experienced in the past. We ended up saving them her time and money, as it allowed the internal people at her company to concentrate on doing what they do best. I'd like to share how we can do the same for you."

Objection example:
"You only offer the B product line and we also need the D product line."

Reply Option 1:
"How important is the D line to you?" In certain situations—and if the prospective sale is big enough—you may want to explore ways to bring in the other line for this customer. But you don't want to invest thousands of dollars just to bring in one line for him if it's not something he really needs or is not of significant importance to him. Here again, you have to ask ⬜uestions so that you have enough knowledge about the company to be able to say, "Based upon what you told me about what you're trying to accomplish, it seems that having the service we provide would benefit more than having the D line because...."

Reply Option 2:
"It is true that we can't supply you with D, but what makes us uni⬜ue is that we've been specializing in manufacturing and distributing B for 20 years...." In this case, you would sell the value of the high quality you are able to maintain in B because it's the only thing you do (as opposed to trying to be all things to

all people). So you might suggest that this customer buys the B line from you, and gets the D products from some-one else.

Reply Option 3:
"We can't supply you with D, but I can suggest someone who can." You can't meet the customer's needs in every case. Sometimes the best thing you can say is, "Based upon what you're looking for, I don't think what we have right now is the best answer to your problem. There is a company that does offer a D product that seems to really fit what you're trying to do right now." Obviously, you don't want to recommend your competitor all the time. But when that is indeed the best solution for the customer, it makes sense. What the customer sees is that you are selling in his or her best interest. That means that when this customer needs a product or a service you do provide, you'll be the one who gets called on first.

Caution: Never knock the competition. If a customer says, "XYZ company can do this for us and you can't," say, "XYZ is a fine company. But let me tell you what makes us unique and different." Go into the strengths of your product that offset the weaknesses of the competition. "We're the only company that can make deliveries to every single one of your locations within a 24-hour time period." When you say you're the only company, you're really pointing out the competitor's weakness without directly putting them down.

Objection example:
"We already have a supplier for your type of product or service."

Reply Option 1:
"That's exactly why I'd like to speak with you. Some of our customers use both our services and the competitor's because we offer different things, but some of them have switched totally to us and here's why...."

Reply Option 2:

"Did you use a different supplier before you had the one you use now? What was the reason you switched to the company you're currently using?" While the customer is exploring those reasons, you may come up with a reason he should switch again, because your company can meet his needs even better than the company he's using now.

What Objections Really Are

Most salespeople think that the worst-case sales scenario is when a customer throws an unexpected objection at you. The truth is, the worst-case scenario is when you hear nothing at all—when the customer just "fades away," doesn't re-turn your phone calls, doesn't reply to your e-mails, cancels the meetings, and you never hear a word of explanation. You haven't made the sale and you don't know why. Chances are you'll never find out.

When a customer expresses an objection, what he or she is really saying is, "I can't buy your product or service be-cause...." When that happens, you've got the greatest sales opportunity in the world. This customer has told you exactly what's holding up the buying decision. All you have to do now is show the customer how the product or service you're offering is not the problem he sees it to be, but instead can benefit him in a variety of ways.

Of course, that's a simplistic view of what happens in real-life sales. In real-life sales, people don't always tell you exactly what their objections are. You often have to dig deep to find them (by following the methods in this book). And in real life, solutions to a customer's problems don't always come to you in a flash of immediate inspiration.

As you read further, you will learn about the most real-life objections salespeople who are developing their business hear, and you'll learn specific techni ues for dealing with them. But there are four things to keep in mind when you're dealing with objections, whatever they might be.

1. Objections are buying signals. When a customer raises an objection, he or she is really saying, "I want to buy your product or service, but I want to get this one problem solved before I go ahead."

2. Objections provide opportunities to better under-stand customers. This includes understanding how they think, how they communicate, what their concerns are, where their priorities lie, and so on. These are all important clues that can help you form better relationships with your customers for immediate sales and for future sales, as well. Often, the one thing that gets you past barriers and through objections is the relationship that is formed between you and the customer.

3. Objections come in many varieties. An objection can be a simple re□uest for missing information. An objection can be a test by someone who wants to see how much you know (or don't know) about his business. It could be a negotiating ploy. An objection can be used to hide the customer's fear of making a mistake. An objection can be the customer's way of saying, "I just don't like you," without coming right out and saying it. It's your job to discover, through the techni□ues you'll find in the rest of this book, just what kind of objection you're really facing.

4. Objections help you move on. Once you have effectively handled an objection, it is time to move on to the next stage of the sales process. If you can't handle the objection, it may be time to move on to another customer.

Eliminating Objections Before They Arise

Whenever I do a sales seminar or training session and get to the part about handling objections, people just go crazy. This is the part they've been waiting for all day. Everyone wants to jump up and say, "Oh boy, have I got one for you. What would you do if somebody gave you this objection…" or, "You woulddon't believe the objection I got the other day…."

They can't wait to tell me how clever they were in answering the objection, or how disappointed they were because they coulddon't get beyond the objection.
Unfortunately, most salespeople I see today are missing the bigger picture. They think that if only they can master handling objections, they'll be meeting their sales quota in no time. They believe (or they've even been taught) that handling objections is accomplished by manipulating the sales process in their favour. Well, I'm here to tell you that the best, most effective way to handle objections has nothing to do with being clever, tricky, or manipulative. The best way to handle objections is to stop them from coming up in the first place, and that is accomplished through the preparation you do before you ever get to the sales call. There are three keys to eliminating objections before they arise:

1. Learn everything there is to learn about your customer, his business, and his industry. Customers want salespeople whose main goal is to understand them and their businesses. They want reps who spend time in pre-call planning. Hence, that they have basic in-formation before they get there and who understand their total environments, their overall industries, and their main competitors. They want to know that the rep is interested in finding out about their goals and objectives (a good sales rep might even help the customer define those goals). You can eliminate a large number of objections by developing a broad range of knowledge—knowledge of the customer's goals and environment, and knowledge of his own product and policies. Customers want to know that you will be able to provide solutions, eliminate head-aches, and help them grow their business. There are some sales reps who show up in front of a customer with five products they've brought in because their managers said, "I want you to push those products." Don't think you can just plop those products in front of the customer and get a "yes" on the spot. It's tempting to go for the ☐uick sale, but

you're better off making sure you understand the customer's goals and strategies and the big picture of what he's trying to do.

2. Match a customer with the product or service that suits him best. Once you've learned who a customer is and what his needs are, your goal is to accommodate those conditions. If your product doesn't ⬜ualify, you may have to walk away from that particular sale. But the only way you can know that for sure is to know your product inside and out. That kind of knowledge enables you to pull information out when you are looking for solutions for customers. You're able to say, "You mentioned that these two factors are most important to you. Well, here's how our product can meet your needs in those areas..." or "Here's how we can help you with this challenge and make it easier for you to...."

3. Fulfil all the steps in the sales cycle. The biggest reason objections arise is because the salesperson is trying to sell the wrong product to the wrong per-son at the wrong time. If you try to close a deal before you know if your customer even needs or wants your product or service, you'll automatically get an objection. If you try to make a sale before you've built a rapport and relationship with that customer, you're leaving yourself wide open. Once in a while, you may get lucky and sail through a sale with no problems at all. But in the long run, there are no shortcuts here. There's an old sales cliché that's true nonetheless: People do business with people they like, trust, and respect. You have to earn each one of those things from your customers.

This kind of preparation re⬜uires focus, concentration, and hard work. However, there is a basic truth of life that says what you put into it is what you get back. The rewards you get out of any endeavour depend on the amount of effort you put into it. Sometimes we're afraid of working hard, because we're afraid we won't get the reward in the end. Rewards are sometimes long in coming, but they do come. Most sales-people, who don't achieve as much success as they want to, don't fall short because of lack of ability, but because they gave up too soon or didn't put in 100-percent effort. Those who do achieve success know that it is only concentrated, focused effort that will produce results.

Feel, felt, Found

This is going to be short and sweet. First, I'm going to tell you that "Feel, Felt, Found" is one of the most basic—and most applicable— methods of diffusing an objection that ever existed. It's one that can be used in almost any sales situation.
Next, I'm going to tell you not to use Feel, Felt, and Found— at least, not in its exact form. It's one of those things that has become such a staple techni□ue for handling objections that it has actually become a cliché. Not that it doesn't work; you just have to be careful how you use it.

I use it myself. I used it all the time in 2013 when I was selling online advertising. Here's how it went:

Objection example:

"I'm sorry, but we don't buy online advertising. We find it doesn't work for us."

Reply: "I can appreciate how you feel."
"A lot of people i've spoken with felt that way too."
"But when they found out how many people they could reach by advertising in our platform, they were amazed. So I'd like to see if there's an opportunity to do the same for you. Would you be interested in an impression ad, or would a conversion campaign be better for you?"
After you fully understand the objection, you can go on to Feel, Felt, Found.

This three-step method can actually be applied to just about any objection you might hear, by the gatekeeper or by anyone else you're dealing with. You just change the third part so that it applies to the particular objection. For ex-ample, if you were dealing with a price objection, you might say, "...when they found out how much money they saved by using our product (or service), they were amazed. I'd like to do the same for you. How is this Thursday morning for me to come in and talk to you about it? Or would the afternoon be better?"

Use It, Don't Abuse It

There's nothing wrong with using Feel, Felt, and Found when it's appropriate. Just don't overuse it. Clearly, you can't use it to handle more than one objection in a sales call. Customers are a lot savvier than they used to be, and many of them know about Feel, Felt, Found too.

In most cases, what you really want to do is ask questions to get your customers to reveal more about their objections. When you use Feel, Felt, Found, you never get beyond the surface of the objection, and you're not addressing the deeper issues behind a customer's concerns.

This is another one of the "foundation" principles: Learn the Feel, Felt, Found method so well that you can use it with-out really using it. Find different ways to say it; adapt it any way that makes sense for your kind of sale.

In the next several chapters, you'll find the most common objections salespeople get and how to handle them. You can use the Feel, Felt, Found method with any type of objection.

Just remember that it is no substitute for asking ☐uestions, ☐ualifying, and following all the other steps of the sales cycle. It's just another tool to keep in your objection-handling arsenal.

Confidence: the great objection deflector

If you've ever watched an Olympic competition, you've seen the faces of champions reflect not only the hard work and preparation that's gone into that moment, but also the confidence they have going into the arena. That confidence is not just what carries them through, it's what communicates their position before the event even starts. They cannot win without this confidence. Their competitors can sense fear, insecurity, and unpreparedness, just as a customer can sense these things in a salesperson who doesn't feel confident. Once they sense a lack of confidence, it makes it easier for them to bring up objections, and more difficult to answer them.

Here are three things you can do to build, maintain, and project the confidence you need:

Prepare. When you walk into calls, you have to have done your homework, studied your customers' businesses, talked to their customers, read their annual reports, and know what problems they have before they're even aware of them.
To understand the importance of preparation, think about your days in school. Some people are not very successful students. They don't know how to study, or they don't understand the value of studying. Then, when test time rolls around, they dread taking the exam because they're so afraid of failure. Those who realize the value of doing homework and being pre-pared for every class and every exam are able to walk in to every test with confidence, knowing they have done as much as they possibly could to make this a positive experience.

That's, the kind of confidence, you need when you're walking into a sales call or meeting. Your success depends 99 percent on your attitude going in. If you're hesitant, customers will see right through that before you even pull out your notebook. Suppose you're confident, based on the amount of preparation you've put in. In that case, you eliminate many of the objections customers would have had if they suspected a lack of knowledge on your part. And because you've done your homework, you'll be much more effective at handling the objections that do come up. You'll be calmer, because you know the answers. You can let the customer talk, then pause, relax, get your thoughts together, and answer based on everything you learned about them.

When I want to prepare to make a sales call, here's what I do: I go to the customer's Website and print out some of the materials I find there. I search the Internet for information and articles about the company to try and find out what the customer is doing successfully and where some of his weaknesses may lie. I also look for general information about the industry if it's one I haven't sold to before. If I can, I talk to other people who are involved in or knowledgeable about their industry and who might be able to give me insights about what's essential to that kind of company. I write down some questions I would like to ask the customer and think about ꓷuestions he might possibly have for me. By the time I get to the sales call, I'm confident that I'm as prepared as I can be for this sales call—no matter what objections I may encounter.

Another reason I am confident when I go into sales calls is because I visualize a successful outcome.

One thing that great achievers have in common—no matter what their field or occupation—is the ability to visualize their goals and dreams. They have a clear, focused picture of their picture that they strive to-ward, no matter what obstacles may appear before them. That doesn't mean they always reach their goals or that they turn out 100 per cent the way they visualized them to be. But they never lose their ability to sustain a positive vision of the future, and the belief that their visions will pull them forward and make them strong.

That vision, plus your preparation, will allow you to fill your presentation with extra details customized to the customer's business. There's an old saying that goes, "Luck happens when preparation meets opportunity." When you walk into an account with that kind of excessive preparation, you exude a quiet confidence and strength in the way you walk, in your handshake, and in the way you look into picture that they strive to-ward, no matter what obstacles may appear before them. That doesn't mean they always reach their goals or that they turn out 100 percent the way they visualized them to be. But they never lose their ability to sustain a positive vision of the future, and the belief that their visions will pull them forward and make them strong.

That vision, plus your preparation, will allow you to fill your presentation with extra details customized to the customer's business. There's an old saying that goes, "Luck happens when preparation meets opportunity." When you walk into an account with that kind of excessive preparation, you exude a ⬜uiet confidence and strength in the way you walk, in your handshake, and in the way you look into
You should always be prepared with at least three factors that separate you from the crowd. Use your knowledge of the customer and your knowledge of your product and service to develop those three key factors, and they will enable you to make your presentation from a position of unassailable strength.

When it comes to selling, many words and phrases are tossed casually about. You've probably heard the phrase "value-added selling" dozens of times. But do you really know what it means? It means more than focusing on the value of your product and the service behind it, but also on the value that you personally bring to the sale.

Successful salespeople are not content to do what every other salesperson does for their customers. They go beyond. They are constantly asking them-selves and their customers, "What else can I offer?" If adding value for your customers is not a high priority for you, you will not be able to compete in today's marketplace. Every time you turn around, there is another product out on the market that is just like yours—exactly like yours. Where, then does your value lie?

It lies within you. You must be the final deciding factor that makes a prospect choose your product over all the others. Even if your prospect doesn't buy from you right away, let her know that, when you call again (or write or send an e-mail or any other communication), it will be to hook into her goals and challenges. You may even have an opportunity to introduce that customer to someone who can help her business—even if it has no immediate benefit for you. Your payoff will come later, when the customer needs your type of service and, be-cause of your consistency in bringing added value, calls you for the business.

A value-added approach to selling puts you in a whole new light for your customers. You become one of their company's greatest assets, one that they will not trade in easily for another vendor or a lower price. It all comes down to three of the most powerful words in the English language, "Yes I Can." Years ago, in one of his audio programs, Earl Nightingale told a story about a team of six American mountain climbers at the bottom of a mountain. A psychologist doing a survey asked each of them one ▢uestion: "Can you make it to the top?" Five of the climbers answered with variations of, "i've been training for this for years. I'll make the best effort possible." One climber, however, answered simply, "Yes I can." Not only was he the first to the mountaintop, because of inclement weather, he was the only one.

There is something about the power of confidence that can move mountains; once we understand this in selling, 90 percent of all obstacles vanish before we even begin to climb.

Five Ways to Differentiate Yourself From the Competition

In order to woo a customer away from a competitor, you have to ask yourself these □uestions: What can I offer that's different from my competitor? What can I offer to bring more business to my customer's business? What value does my product or service have that can add value to the customer's business?
Here are five proven ways to differentiate yourself from the competition:

1. Superior Service. Service is what keeps you in business for the long haul. It's your track record that builds your current customers' confidence in you, and attracts prospects to you. You've got to be able to say, "Try us, and we'll prove that we will consistently do what no one else will." Differentiation comes through outrageous service, and that outrageous service adds value in the eyes of the customer.

2. Uni□ue Value. The best way to bring extra value to your customers is to understand their businesses better than anyone else out there. Get to know the companies, the people involved, and the industry as a whole. It's your knowledge that will be the differentiating factor. When I do seminars, for example, I don't just do a needs analysis with the people who hire me. I spend many hours on the phone, not just with their salespeople, but with my customers' customers as well. I interview their customers on tape and play back some of the comments during the seminar. These customers tell the salespeople what they're doing right and what they're not doing that the customers would appreciate. This is something different that makes me uni□ue and gives more value to my seminar.

The concept of adding value applies no matter what you sell. Every time you go into an organization and ask questions about the company's needs and goals, you have another opportunity to look for ways you can support their vision. A value-added approach to selling puts you in a whole new light for your customers. You become one of their company's assets, one that they will not trade in easily for an-other vendor.

3. Customization. When I get information from my customer's customer, it allows me to tailor my pro-gram directly to my customer's needs and concerns.
That's what every customer is seeking. Even though your product or service may be similar to others on the market, it's your job to make it as customer-specific as possible. The best companies have their R and D people calling customers constantly to find out how they're using their products, what they like about them, what they don't like, what would they change, and how they would make them easier to use. Old products are then modified and new products are designed to match the information gleaned from these customers. No matter what you sell—whether it's a product or a service— your differentiating factor should evolve from the knowledge and input you get from your end users.

4. Selling Through. In business to business, your real job is to be a sales rep for your customers. Your objective is to help them sell more of whatever they sell. The more you help your customers sell, the more they're going to order from you. You sell through by showing your customers how your product can provide solutions to their challenges. You can also help them sell by "bridging," connecting XYZ company with ABC company— even if you have no stake in pairing the two. For instance, if I'm selling a product to the XYZ Advertising Specialty Company, I might refer them to ABC company (an organization I know uses advertising specialties) even if my product is not involved. But just by introducing the two companies, I become a valuable—and differentiated—asset to both.

5. Building Solid Relationships. Striving for the previous four factors will definitely help you rise above the product parity that is so prevalent today. But the most important differentiating factor of all is who you are and how you connect with your customers. That's what makes you uni□ue. How many times have you heard of a salesperson leaving one company to join another and having all his customers go with him? That's because each one of those customers had a special bond with that salesperson that was stronger than the bond to the particular product he sold.

If you want to impress potential customers, load up with ammunition that separates you from your competitors. You don't need to spend money on colour and flash for your presentations or perform outrageous stunts to get noticed. You do need to have two or three major points that demonstrate your unique value, and you need to do your homework so that your information is heavily focused on their goals and challenges. Stick to the basics. If you want to stand head and shoulders above the crowd, just remember to start from a solid foundation of service, value, and strong relationships.

10 mistakes that annoy customers and incite objections

If you want to know how to be a successful salesperson, there is one person who knows better than anyone else: your customer. Treat a customer well and you'll end up with a loyal buyer. But treat a customer badly and you'll run into more objections than you could ever imagine.
As I've said before, everyone makes mistakes. And for the most part, customers are a pretty forgiving bunch. But that only goes so far. Customers find some mistakes so annoying that they get in the way of doing business section includes ten of them.

Mistake Number 1: Not Being Organized

This is really common sense. No customer wants to sit there and wait while you look through all your papers for the one piece of information you were sure you brought with you but now can't seem to find anywhere. Some salespeople feel they can wing it—that they can go into a sales call "blind" and still be effective and persuasive. They think their charm will win the day.

But charm only goes so far. If the customer sees that you're unprepared for a meeting, he won't have much faith that you will be prepared to take care of his account. You've lost any credibility you might have had.
Customers don't mind if you don't have a ready answer to a question they throw at you. They'd rather you be honest and tell them, "I don't know the answer to that. Let me go back to office and do some research, and I'll give you a call tomorrow." But they do mind if you waste their time by saying, "I have that information with me. Wait a minute, I think I left in the car. No, wait, it should be here in my briefcase. Didn't I give that to you already? No? Okay, I'll e-mail you the info later."

When you have all the information about your prospect collected and organized before your meeting, when you have done your homework, talked to people, studied your product line, and know it inside out—when you have everything in order—not only do you make a much better impression, your clarity of thinking is much better as well. Your direction, your purpose, and your focus is much stronger, so you exude confidence when you walk in the door.

Mistake Number 2: Talking Too Much

If you've read many books about sales, you might get the impression that all you're supposed to do is ask questions and listen to the answers. Obviously, you have to talk at some point—you do eventually have to answer a customer's objections, and to present your product's features and benefits and demonstrate how they meet the customer's needs. For instance, you might answer an objection about poor service performance in the past by saying, "I can appreciate that, but we now have a whole new strategy in place to deal with service issues, which I know are important to you. Here's how it works...."

Customers get annoyed, however, when you just talk about your product without knowing what it is about your product or service that might be important to them. If you are prone to talking too much, try this in your next meeting. Sit back, and as the customer is talking, pull out a notepad and start taking notes. Listen to what the customer is saying, and how she's saying it. Tune in to what she's saying. Have the customer talk about what's important to her.

Throw questions back to her: "Cheryl, you mentioned this is something you tried in the past with your company. Can you go into that a little more?" Or, "I heard you just introduced a new line. How's that going? What's your biggest challenge in getting that out on the market?" Be aware of how much you're talking before you've gathered all the information you need. If you're doing all the talking, that means you're not listening or learning. The customer will feel— and rightly so—that you're more interested in making the sale than in helping her find a solution. When you find you're talking too much, ask a question, sit back, and listen.

Mistake Number 3: Interrupting

Sometimes when a customer voices his concern, you can't help but get excited about the fact that your product or service can provide what you see as the perfect solution, and you want to let the customer know about it. So, you interrupt and jump right in even before the customer has finished speaking. This is not only rude, it's dangerous. The customer will, of course, be annoyed that he was not allowed to finish his thought. What if the end of his thought had been, "…and that's why I want to place an order from you," and you cut him off before he could get there? More likely, as we discussed in the six-step method, you'll bring in a whole new objection the customer had never even considered. Let the customer finish speaking. Take a deep breath and take in what he's just said. Think about a response that makes sense. A pause is not only a courtesy to customers because it lets them speak their minds, but it also gives you time to prepare the right come-back, the right ⬜uestion, or the right solution for them.

Mistake Number 4: Lacking Sincerity

Sincerity comes from embracing and believing in what you are doing. When you are sincere, you are not false, hypocritical, or deceitful. Customers look for these ⬜ualities in salespeople, as well as earnestness, truth, candour, and frankness. They want to do business with people who are real, genuine, honest, straightforward, and trustworthy. When you believe in what you're doing, and you're truly there to serve the customer's best interest, you don't have to try to be sincere. You don't have to try to be excited. It comes out naturally. If you're not really sincere about what you're selling, you'd probably be better off doing some-thing else. You can have all the skills and steps in this book working for you, but if a customer senses you're not sincere, that will come through louder than any words you can say. When you are sincere, however, your true self comes through and you allow the customer to connect with you the person, not the salesperson.

Mistake Number 5: Not Analysing Needs

When you're asking ⬜uestions and you're really listening, you're learning things that are going to help you solve your customer's problems. If you are not asking questions and establishing need, you're doing nothing but presenting another gadget that's going to give the customer a headache. It takes an effective needs analysis to come up with solutions that overshadow the objections that concern your customers.

Mistake Number 6: Being Too Pushy

Customers often complain about salespeople who are too pushy and who try to "convince" them they need a product or service that doesn't fit their business or answer their needs. The truth is, you can't really convince anyone to purchase anything. What you can do is make it worthwhile for this customer to make a positive buying decision by demonstrating the value of what you're selling.
You're being pushy and aggressive when your only goal is to make a sale and the customer's concerns don't matter to you. You're being pushy when you make the customer feel wrong or guilty for stating her concerns or asking questions. You're being assertive when you believe 100 percent in your product or service and that what you're selling can be of benefit to this customer. You're being effective when you respect the customer's right to object.

There's often a fine line between being aggressive and being assertive. There's nothing wrong with pushing your idea. But when the customer sees that you're pushing solely for your own interest, when there's no understanding of the customer's point of view, that's when you'll get "stalling" objections: "I have to think about it," or "I have to consult my partner about this."

One of my partners is also one of the greatest salespeople I know. He is very soft spoken, he listens to customers, and he's always calm and low-key. Customers see him almost as a father figure. But he sells. When he says some-thing, he says it with great authority: "Here's what we're going to do…." He has a quiet strength that customers respect. He also lets his customers know, even when they're voicing concerns that he is totally on their side. Customers don't look to him as a salesman—they look to him for answers.

Mistake Number 7: Reciting a Script

We've all run into them at one time or another—the salesperson who gives you the sense that if you interrupt his pitch, you ruin his whole presentation. Maybe you're in a meeting with a salesperson and the phone rings. You take the call, and when you get back to the salesperson and say, "Sorry for the interruption. Go on," he begins at the beginning again or takes up exactly where he left off. The presentation sounds like something he's prepared verbatim. It's fine to prepare an outline of where you're going and what you're trying to accomplish. In fact, that's critical. When I talk with my partners about going into a meeting, for in-stance, we prepare beforehand what we're going to talk about, how we're going to present our ideas, what we will do in various scenarios. We do this in general terms. We don't know exactly what we're going to say, but we know we can rely on our overall knowledge and our specific preparation for this meeting.

The most successful salespeople are great on their feet. When they're thrown curve balls and objections in a meeting, they can handle them and get back on track. You don't want your training to show. It becomes a turnoff. You must treat each customer individually and have enough confidence in your knowledge and skills to know that you will be able to handle the situation without planning exactly what you're going to say.

Mistake Number 8: Not Building Rapport

Everybody wants to buy from someone he likes, trusts, and respects. Customers have to feel comfortable with you. This means that they find you agreeable to deal with and take pleasure in your company. You don't have to become best friends with every prospect or customer, but within the con-text of buyer/seller interactions, customers want to know that you are friendly, respectful, considerate, and accommodating. They trust you when they have confidence that you're there in their best interest (as well as your own—they know you're there to sell them something). This is a trust that you earn as you go, from your initial meeting through the closing of the sale, as well as through customer service and follow-through. They respect you when they see that you are an expert in your field with a thorough knowledge of their company and industry.

Customers want to see who you are. If you try to "act like a salesperson," customers will see right through you. They want to make a connection with you so that they can feel good about buying from you. If they don't trust you and don't feel comfortable with you, they will bring up more objections—and the objections will be harder to handle.

Mistake Number 9: Getting Defensive

If I told you that I've never gotten defensive in a sales call, I would by lying. When you believe in your product or service strongly and believe that it can truly benefit customers, it is only natural to get defensive if somebody ⬜uestions that product or doesn't see the benefit. We want to defend what we believe in. However, when you get defensive, what you actually display is a lack of confidence. That's when you start feeling that you have to keep talking to try to convince and persuade and push that customer into seeing things your way. That never works. Perhaps there is information about the customer that you've missed. Per-haps the customer has misunderstood something you've said about your product or service. Perhaps you've tried to close before you've established rapport. Whatever the reason, when you get defensive, you end up arguing with the customer. When that happens, you have al-ready lost. Instead, take a deep breath and ask ⬜uestions about why the customer feels the way he does: "Can you go into more detail about your concerns?" That way, you can gain a better understanding of the customer's problem, and give yourself time to think about how you're going to come back with a proper explanation to settle his uneasiness.

Mistake Number 10: Taking It Personally

Let's face it. Salespeople, like entrepreneurs, actors, and writers—in fact, most people—face rejection every day. Whatever you're doing in life, there are going to be some people who just don't like you, who disagree with you, or who don't think what you're doing or what you're selling is important. When you face that kind of rejection, there are three things you can do.

Your first choice is to ignore it, which is difficult.

At best. If you're good at sales, you take pride in what you do, you have confidence and enthusiasm, and you don't like being turned down.

The second kind of reaction is to let rejection motivate you. That's what I do. First, I look at where the rejection is coming from. Who is the "rejector"? How knowledge-able is he? How much does he know you as an individual and what you can do? I might even call him back to find out just what the problem is: "Can you help me understand exactly what is it that is stopping us from moving forward or what it is that's holding you back?" Maybe it's some-thing I can fix or solve. At least it gives me an opportunity to solve it; doing nothing leaves me at a dead end. In that way, objections become a motivating factor and not an obstacle.

The worst way to deal with rejection is to let it get to you and start believing what the other person is saying. Successful salespeople know it's not the rejection that's important, it's what we do with it. Particular situations may get them down, but they will not let those situations take them out of the game. If they can't get to a difficult prospect today, they make a long-term plan to keep trying to make contact over the next six months or a year. If a great deal falls through, they study what went wrong and improve their approach for the next time. If they can't change a situation, they change their attitude about it.

They don't let—they won't let—the world defeat them. The world will never defeat you, if you have confidence in yourself and your abilities. In the next section, you'll learn that confidence is one of the strongest weapons you'll ever have against any obstacles that arise.

Knowing when to walk away

Is it ever appropriate to answer an objection by saying, "You know what? I have to agree with you here. My product (or service) and your company are not a great match. Thanks for your time"? Salespeople are taught—in fact, they're drilled on the saying—"Never take no for an answer." Never give up. Keep trying until you find a way to get through. That's good advice—most of the time. But there are those times when it is appropriate for salespeople to walk away from potential business, times when no is the only appropriate answer.

Another basic business "truth" we've heard since the beginning of business is that the customer is always right. And, for the most part, that is also true. But there are times when it's appropriate to tell a particular buyer—the one who saps your strength and wastes your time again and again— that although the customer may be right, the relationship is wrong.

I'm not saying to get rid of every customer who is difficult to deal with. I'm suggesting that it may be time to weed out your customer base so that you can harvest the greatest re-wards. Here are some ways to do that:

Know when to walk away. Persistence is a value-added ☐uality in selling. But if you've tried again and again to reach a prospect who "doesn't get" your product or service, who doesn't see the value, or with whom you can't establish a connection, it may be time to walk away. If you're being stubbornly persistent about sticking to a path that doesn't lead anywhere, that's counter-productive; you want to spend your time where you're getting results.

Some customers are simply rude and disrespectful. Others may be unrealistically demanding, wanting service that is impossible for you (or anyone else, for that matter) to provide. If this demanding customer is your only prospect, you may feel you have to stick it out. But when you have enough activity going on, you don't have to take business that it is going to produce more headaches than revenue.

Some customers are just not worth the aggravation, for example those who are constantly asking you to do things for them, such as "throw in" extra parts or supplies for free or give them more of a discount. If the customer cannot see the value of your product or service, it's time for you to say no.

Leaving this kind of customer is not a failure; it only shows how much you value your time and product.

Follow the 80/20 rule. Take stock of your customers. Who are the ones giving you most of your business? Who are the ones giving you most of the headaches? How much time are you spending with each?

Of your total business, 80 percent comes from only 20 percent of your customers; focus on those customers that have the highest potential of increasing your bottom line. You must make a realistic evaluation of the cost of doing business with a high maintenance customer. If someone demands constant attention and a huge amount of work for very little return, you won't be able to spend □uality time with other customers who may be bringing in a higher profit.

Ask the difficult □uestions. Too many salespeople are "stuck" with problem customers, because they don't ask the hard questions. They get sucked into a long, drawn-out sales process, because they have never asked, "Is there anyone else who is involved in making this decision?" They spend a lot of time with an indecisive customer because they haven't asked, "What's our next step?" Or "What do we need to do to reach a decision by the end of this month?" They're afraid of rejection, afraid of objections. But getting an objection is often the only way to truly understand how the customer is thinking and get the sale back on track—or realize that this track is not the right one for you or your customer to follow.

Ask yourself some difficult ☐uestions. For instance, "Am I presenting to the right person?" If the answer is no, it may not be possible at this point to go over his head and get to the decision-maker. Then ask yourself "Have I done everything I could? Do I understand the customer's needs? Have I presented a strong solution? What is it that's holding them back? Could it be that he just doesn't like me?" That is always a possibility. After all, try as we might, there are some customers with whom we just can't make a connection. That's when it's time to ask yourself, "Is it better to cut my losses now and move on the next account?"

Measure your return on investment (ROI). How do you know when it's time to end the relationship? First, you have to know what your value is. You have to have the confidence and belief in yourself and your product or service to be able to say, "I can spend this amount of time with this customer, and no more. I can sell my product or service for this price, and no less." Then, you have to take the time to do a thorough and honest ROI analysis. How many times have you called on this customer without moving the sale forward? Is the time you're putting into this account worth what you're getting back?

Leave the door open. Never lock the door behind you when you go. There's no point in telling a customer, "You're not worth my time." Say instead, "I appreciate the time you've invested with me, but it doesn't look like this is a good match for us." You might even recommend another product or ser-vice you think might fit his or her needs. Try to walk away on friendly terms so that both of you have the option to call again, if the situation should change.

The next time you deal with a difficult customer, ask yourself this question: "Is the time that I'm taking with this customer taking time away from others who need me more?" If the answer is yes, then it's time to cut your losses and walk away. If your first thought is to say, "the customer is always right," stop and ask yourself, "is this customer right for me?"

PART 2

Effective counters will grow your Business

If you are in a business-to-business sales role, including retention sales, inside or outside, account management, consultative, transactional commodity, or value selling, this book will help you increase your sales income. Sales professionals make their living convincing buyers to convince themselves they need a product or service. The sky is the limit on income potential (not to mention the freedom we experience being out and about and not sitting behind a desk all day). However, not every month is a great month for sales and commissions. This means that with just about every deal, you will encounter people who just say no or maybe. You need to answer customer objections effectively in order to turn nos and maybes into more yeses to ensure your future income.

This book will help you overcome the most common sales objections i've seen. Sales objections are part of your selling success. And since selling success is your goal, choose to be exceptional at answering buyer objections. Answering objections is something you learn to love because your financial income depends on your ability to navigate ￼uickly through them. Developing the ability to respond quickly to objections will help you stabilize and grow your income.

There are millions of salespeople on the streets right now trying to sell their goods and services. There are millions of phone calls being placed right now in hopes of getting an appointment or moving a deal forward toward a decision.

Keep this in mind while making your own sales calls. Prospects, buyers, and gatekeepers have their own work to get done, and unless you have a compelling reason to meet with them, they will object to your re□uest.

Every stage of the sales process is filled with objections from the prospect or current customer. When you get a prospect on the phone and ask for a meeting, you'd better anticipate objections. When you ask for an order to close a deal, you'd better anticipate objections—for example, when you're networking at an event, trying to get the decision maker to meet with you. You'd better anticipate and expect objections.

Anticipate and expect objections, because they are coming

It's a soon-to-be financially broke salesperson that doesn't anticipate an objection. A linebacker on a football team anticipates the hit and therefore is ready for the impact. A jet pilot anticipates turbulence when in flight and therefore isn't surprised when the plane bounces around. In a like manner, you need to anticipate and be ready for objections. Every objection is a defensive hit. Effectively countering objections is an opportunity to change the buyer's mind-set, so be ready.

As a salesperson and now a communicator of sales strategies, I am fre□uently surprised by how many really good salespeople do not spend time developing their ability to negotiate a sales objection. Many think they will be ready the moment an objection

51

happens. When a prospect says, "I have a better price from another vendor" or "Let me think about it," they answer without thinking.

Salesperson: "So let's move this deal forward."

Prospect: "I have a better price from another vendor."

Salesperson: "Oh, okay ... Let me knock off another 20 percent."

Prospect: "Let me think about it."

Salesperson: "Okay, you think about it, and I will call you next week."

Prospect: "No, I will call you."

Salesperson: "Okay, call me when you're ready."

This is tragic! These ridiculous responses cost you and your company time and money, which causes you to lose deals and personal income—not to mention how much harder you will have to work.

Do you really want to work harder? I hope not. This is why I wrote this book: to help you respond to objections effectively and ☐uickly.

How to use this book

I have identified 70 of the most difficult and typical types of objections, along with suggested counters. To get you started, consider these six important "Steps"

Step One: Anticipate Objections

You need to anticipate that the prospect will push back and object. Make it your goal to develop a superior objection-countering mind-set. This mind-set prepares you for future sales objections. You can't know what the customer is thinking, but you can anticipate their objections and be ready to respond. Anticipating objections will cause your mind to think and practice possible conversations before they happen. Much as a musician practices before performing for an audience or a football team practices before a game, when you anticipate objections, you prepare yourself to be able to counter them.

Step Two: Learn to Minimize and Redirect Objections

If you anticipate sales objections, you will be able to quickly and efficiently minimize them. Minimizing is the art of making prospects' objections appear insignificant to them and also making the objections not the only issue. You will be more confident and will not freeze when customers push back at you. Be ready to negotiate the conversation so that you and your clients can discover why your product or service is a good fit for them.

Step Three: Role-Play

If you anticipate that a prospect is going to object, you should be writing down possible objections and role-playing. You can minimize and redirect those objections only through effective role-playing.
For example, when boxers anticipate punches, they are better able to minimize the impact of the hits—and, in many cases, avoid a knockout. However, imagine if they didn't spend time preparing. The dream of winning big would be just a dream. This is the same principle when dealing with sales objections. Practice through role-playing. You will be able to naturally and comfortably counter every objection like a possible hit, minimize the impact, and win the match.

Step Four: Choose to Improve Your Personal Skill Set

Invest in your own education. Use this book as a guide to improve your personal skills at answering customer objections. You may be working as an entrepreneur or independent agent and need to fund your own education. This book is your best resource. I suggest a steady diet of reading and practicing by using this book daily.

Step Five: Get a Workout Buddy

Another successful method is to find someone who also wants to improve his or her skills and can meet fre□uently with you for your own personal objection workshop. Practice until you can respond □uickly and effectively.

Step Six: Inspire Sales Team Discussions

Sales managers can use this book for coaching and development in sales meetings. Take one or two sales objections, and offer them up for discussion in your sales meetings.
Remember—the more you practice, the better able you are to handle sales objections effectively.

Objections shouldn't be arm-wrestling matches

Answering sales objections doesn't mean arm wrestling a prospect until you win. If people are interested in what you're selling, in most cases they're going to offer some kind of objection. When the customer raises an objection, don't start an arm-wrestling match.

I was in a mall during the holiday season, browsing around while my daughter and son were doing what teenagers do: shopping with the money Dad gave them. I was standing in front of a clothing store, looking at seasonal fashions for men, when I heard a woman trying to get the attention of a shopper.

"Hey, mister … hey … you."
I turned slightly to my right and looked over my shoulder, and I realized I was the person she was talking to.

"Are you talking to me?" I asked.
"Yes," the salesperson said, smiling. "Do you need a new cell phone?"

This is when I realized I was being solicited by a cell phone salesperson in a kiosk in the middle of the aisle. Nice person, I thought. Aggressive, friendly, pleasant voice, and she got my attention. I imagine she could have been thinking she was a great salesperson because she possessed certain necessary sales traits. What she may not have realized was how much commission she lost that day because she didn't know how to effectively counter my objection. Let me share with you a few things she didn't know about my cell phone situation.

I've had the same flip cell phone for almost five years. Yes, I know—after one year it's a dinosaur; my kids remind me every time they see me use it. My cell contract is up for renewal, so there's nothing keeping me from upgrading. I'm thinking often of getting an upgrade from my current phone to a new phone. My problem is that I know what every button on my phone does. Having to stop and learn something new is frustrating for me. I'm a creature of habit, so I'm comfortable with my little phone. It's like a family member to me. It's old, but I'm familiar with it.

I don't have e-mail capabilities on my phone, so an upgrade is something I'm interested in. I've found that texting is how my kids prefer to communicate, so a better keyboard would be helpful.

And I'm very frustrated with the cell phone service of the national carrier I use. On top of that, in the middle of a conversation, the cell line often drops. When I say often, I mean every day. The bottom line is that my experience with my cell provider has not been good. So I'm somewhat frustrated.

Do you get the picture now?

I have a need to buy a new phone, and I am unhappy with my current provider. I'm a prime candidate for a new phone order. Now, back to my story.
The salesperson knows nothing about my current cell phone situation, and she works for the cell phone carrier I use. So here is how the conversation went:

Salesperson: "Hey mister … hey … you."
Me: "Are you talking to me?"
Salesperson: "Yes, do you need a new cell phone?"

Me: "Yes, I do."
Salesperson: "Great! We have lots of great deals going on."
Me (interrupting her sales pitch): "Oh yeah, I use your company already, but I do not like your service."
Salesperson: "What? Sure you like our service … We are the best."
Me: "Well, I'm not feeling like you're the best, because I don't like the service I'm getting. The line drops all the time."
Salesperson: "How old is your phone? Maybe you need to upgrade."
Me (very friendly tone): "Miss, I just said I don't care for your service."
Salesperson (very pushy and defensive): "Have you had your phone checked out? I think that's what your problem is. So let's upgrade your phone and get it fixed."
(Now we're arm wrestling.)
Me: "Sorry, but I don't think getting a new phone is the solution to my problem."

I turned and walked away while she was still instructing me on how my problem wasn't their problem.

Can you see how the salesperson, by her inability to counter my objection effectively, lost a current customer who had a need and was very interested in upgrading? I wonder how many potential sales she'd lost in the last sixty days. I expect her approach sent many potential clients to another provider.

• What was it the salesperson could not see?
• Why did she feel that pushing for her point of view would help her make the sale?
• Why didn't she investigate what I needed while anticipating objections?

Here is an example of what the salesperson could have done better:
Salesperson: "Oh, I'm so sorry we aren't meeting your expectations. Can you tell me what's happening?"

Me: "When I am on a call, the line drops. This seems to happen every day."
Salesperson: "I know how frustrating that can be because that happened to me. Have you called the help desk?"

Me: "No, I'm just dealing with it until I find a new vendor."
Salesperson: "We acknowledge there has been a problem with our lines dropping calls. So I apologize for the lack of call ꓓuality. We have added more towers and soon will resolve the problem. If I can have your number, I will look into the situation and call you back with a solution and more information. Until then, are you having any phone issues other than the line dropping?"

Notice how the salesperson didn't ignore my current problem with her company but acknowledged my dissatisfaction with empathy before moving to upgrade my phone. This is the proper way to deal with an objection from a buyer.

Take care of the current frustration. Get the buyer to talk about his or her problem, and try to relate to it before changing the subject. When you do this, the buyer will be more likely to talk about other opportunities.

Make Buying Safe

Make it safe for prospects to talk about their concerns, and they will be open to hearing your solutions. Make it unsafe for the potential client, and she or he will not trust your motive. Trust and respect make the client feel safe. Make it safe for customers to tell you their concerns, and they will be open to your solutions.

Customers who do not trust your true motive will either sugar coat their response or just pretend they're interested. They may also get aggressive and fully enter an arm-wrestling match—or shut down and simply walk away. The salesperson's problem in the example I shared is that she didn't know how to answer a customer objection from the customer's point of view. Prospects with objections are a perfect indicator they want to talk.

Getting an objection from a potential customer is not a bad thing. You want to identify key objections as early as possible. Not all prospects will open their purse and hand you their money without raising some concerns. However, when a prospect or client

offers up an objection …

See the problem from their perspective first. Don't assume you see it from their side and finish their sentence. Don't try to prove them wrong or make them feel like their opinion isn't important.

As the salesperson, expect some pushback and be ready to give an answer quickly, confidently, and politely.

Salespeople who feel they need to arm wrestle prospects simply are not selling. They are pushing potential clients away. Stop and see the world from the prospect's viewpoint, and you will create an atmosphere of trust and respect.

Avoid quota obsession disorder

Most salespeople have a sales quota they need to reach—or some kind of measurement that lets the organization know how effective they are at selling. The problem is that salespeople can become so focused on their quota that they are blind to what actually makes up the quota. This has a bad side effect.

Being obsessed with a quota takes your interest off what the client needs. A prospect can sense when a salesperson's only interest is in getting a commission. Since people act out what they think, such salespeople approach prospects just as a hungry lion approaches a lamb with a broken leg. Making the kill is all they think about.

So what is the key component to selling and answering objections? Building trust and credibility. Where trust is the rudder on a ship, credibility is the sail. These two are important to navigating through client objections. Lose these, and you have no chance of a deal.

Become a skillful negotiator

Answering objections is closely related to being a skilful negotiator. The best way to respond to an objection is to interpret it as a question asking for more information. However, if you react defensively to a prospect's objection, you could be leaving a lot of money lying on the table.

Knowing what to say next when an objection is offered, knowing how to negotiate the conversation, and discovering key customer power points prepares you to answer objections □uickly, comfortably, easily, and effectively.

The first skill you need to develop in order to minimize objections is to learn to listen. Listening is an art form. It's like seeing a picture being painted in front of your eyes, so get your paintbrush ready.

Can you tell when someone is not listening to you? Sure you can. There's an awkward sense when you're having a conversation in which the other party isn't tuned in to what you're saying. What signals your attention that he or she isn't listening? Body language and tone.

A lot has been said about communication—and even more about the art of listening. As a reminder, here are a few key "painter's tools" you'll want to have with you.

• Remember the eighty-twenty rule: either on the phone or in a meeting, the prospect should be talking 80 percent of the time. You should be talking 20 percent of the time. Some think that pushing for a prospect's opinion is persuading, so they talk too much themselves; once they hear an objection, they jump into a presentation. Avoid this.

• Avoid poor listening. Beware of concentrating on what you have to say rather than on what the other person is saying.

• Avoid emotional filters. They distort what is really being said. When you get emotional, you aren't logical. When you aren't logical, you tend to draw □uick conclusions.

Attentive listening involves the following:

• Be motivated to listen. Lean forward, and tune everything out except what clients say. Listen to what they mean more than to the actual words used.

• When you speak, it's better to ask ⬚uestions concerning their objections. For example, when the salesperson heard I was frustrated with her company's service, she could have said, "Oh, I am so sorry we aren't meeting your expectation. Please tell me what has been happening."

• Do not interrupt a prospect midsentence.

• Fight distractions.

• Do not trust your memory; write down key things the prospect says.

• Maintain eye contact. Looking away communicates a lack of interest.

• React to the message, not to the person you're speaking with. When prospects say, "I have a better price from another competitor" or "I don't like your service," stay calm and really listen to the purpose or meaning behind what they are saying. If you react emotionally, the buyer takes control of the sale.

• Clarify what you heard the prospect say.

• Verify whether what you think is fact or fiction.

• Reflecting empathy about the prospect's concerns and issues is the first act of business. If you do this first, the prospect will open up to you and your solution.

Why do customers stall?

Understanding the buyer's perspective will help you discover why customers stall and object in the first place. Buyers or prospects have their own perspectives on what their needs and wants are. Knowing how to manage their perspectives puts you in a strong position to answer their objections.

Why does a prospect stall? Here are some of the hidden reasons:

• The prospect wants a high-quality product at a fair and reasonable price.

• The prospect feels competent and has good taste. You want to respect this and act accordingly.

• The prospect would like to avoid risk and trouble.

• The prospect wants to look good for the organization.

• The prospect wants relief from unnecessary work.

• The prospect has a problem and needs a solution.

• The prospect doesn't want to change the status quo.

The salesperson, on the other hand, has a different perspective. You want to make a commission. All salespeople want this, but being good at answering objections means we need to approach prospects from their perspective.

A simple statement that diffuses objections

A very good friend of mine shared with me how he ☐uickly diffuses objections. He simply answers almost every objection with this statement: "That's perfect! That's why I'm here!"

Here are a few examples:

Prospect: "I already have this service!"

Salesperson: "That's perfect because that's why I'm here."

Prospect: "I'm already under contract."

Salesperson: "That's perfect. That's why I'm here!"

Prospect: "We have already had a salesperson from your company call on us."

Salesperson: "That's perfect because that's why I'm here."

When I first heard this statement, I just laughed. Could it be that easy? For a few weeks after hearing about it, I started using it as a primer for answering objections.
Honestly, it worked. In fact, it worked so well I now encourage you to use this simple statement as a starter sentence to counter every objection.

You don't think it will work?

"That's perfect … and that's why I'm here!"

Part three: the 70 Objections

On the following pages, you'll find 70 sales objections and how to easily counter them.

The "Don't Say" sections list some very honest counters i've heard from salespeople in the field. You may have heard some as well. Some are very funny!

If you're like me and get bored easily, you don't want to read a lot of narrative. So I made this section ⬜uick and to the point.

1. "I want to think it over."

How would you counter this objection?

Say:
• I understand. You want to make the best decision. What do you feel you need to think about?

• I can see that. Tell me—is it money that concerns you?

• What questions have I not answered for you?

• What part of my proposal would you like to think over?

• Can you be honest with me? You said this won't meet your needs. Am I missing something?

• Listen—really smart people can tell this is a good deal. And you did say you thought this solution would meet your needs. Didn't you say that? Don't lie to me now! I have met with six people today, and they all said the same thing as you. So unless you are just a big fat liar, I suggest you level with me.

• Mr. Customer, it's the end of the month. If I don't meet my ⬜uota by five today, my boss is going to be really mad, and I just may lose my job. I have nine kids all under the age of seven. Do you want me to lose my job? Let's not think it over any more. Let's say yes!

You need t   ‹ly; don't blink
or hesitate.   asonable
sounding re   edback, and
the messag   ‹is idea,
product, or

Objections ‹   to ask more
uestions.   and then
use one of t   ur answer,
and get com   ›n you.

2. "Your pr‹ ....sıve than your competitor's."

Say

• I agree we are not the low-price leader. Are you looking for a company that can offer you only the lowest price possible, or are service and uality a concern?

• Many of my clients said the same thing until we took a closer look at what features and benefits they were getting compared to what I'm offering. Can we go through the benefits of each and discover what features are best for your business?

Don't Say:

• Well, duh. Of course we are. Don't you want to get the best bang for your buck? I mean, who am I competing with anyway? … Oh, them. Well, they really suck, and rumours have it they are heading into big financial problems.

• I don't like to spread rumors, but I heard that the vendor you're using is under a government investigation. Don't you think switching now is a good idea? I do! Here's a pen. Just sign right here.

Imagine you are the prospect and you asked a salesperson this question. Why would you ask it? Place yourself in his or her shoes and think about what's going on. People buy products all the time that cost more money than others. I know I do. So the prospect is saying, "Hey, I don't see the cost value, and my need for the product isn't motivating me enough to buy from you."

Find out first from your prospects how the product will help them do something better or faster. Then use what they said when they ask this classic objection.

People buy from people they like. So use exceptional relationship skills to tip the decision scale your way. Tell the prospect, "Yes, you're right. We do charge more money, and here is why …" Approach the client like a consultant problem solver. You'll find it easier to fire back a reply if you and the prospect are both interviewing each other to see if there is a good reason to do business together.

3. "We aren't interested."

Say:

• I can understand you not being interested on the basis of a phone call. However, we've helped many companies like yours reduce costs and improve their market size. That's the reason for getting together. I would like to introduce myself and learn more about you. I promise not to take much of your time. Can we meet for a few minutes? How is Tuesday at ten o'clock or Thursday at nine o'clock?

• Mr. Owner, I specialize in helping people in your position gain more market share using our product and service. I was just wondering if you would be interested in getting together for a few minutes to learn more about you and your business and to see if it makes sense to do business together.

Don't say:

• You can be happy the day you sign with our competitor because of the price, or you can be happy today with the □uality of our product (or service) when you sign with us. It's your choice. But don't blame me when things don't work out.

• Sure, you're not interested. I mean, you don't know me. You think I'm just a stupid salesperson. But you are interested in saving money, right? Hello? Are you there?
If you don't create interest with prospects, why would they want to waste their time meeting with you? Creating interest in meeting with you can be frustrating when you're focused on what you want and not what the prospect wants.

I'm sure you've had salespeople try to educate you on why you need to meet with them, how great their product is, and how many clients are happy with their services; however, prospects don't really care about you, your product, or your company. They care about what you, your product, or your company can do for them. The rule for answering this objection is not to get the objection in the first place.

Think about this:

You are a small-business owner of a company that makes candles. As the owner, it's all about gaining market share. You want to get more customers and keep them. You get a call from a salesperson, who asks you, "Mr. Owner, I am Stepp with ABC Company. We are the best in the industry, and we can help you make more candles."

The point is, owners have heard this before, and you're keeping them from doing something they feel is more important than listening to another sales pitch. They feel salespeople are annoying. However, if the salesperson said, "Mr. Owner, I specialize in helping people in your position gain more market share using our product and service. I was wondering if you would be interested in …"

Now the owner is as interested as a toddler with his eye on the ice cream truck coming down the street.

4. "We are happy with our current vendor."

Say:

• Great, may I ask you what they do that you're happy with?

• I understand that these things are important to you. Do you think having a backup vendor would be helpful in the event your current supplier doesn't come through?

• That's great. Are you aware of the changes in the industry? New features? New benefits?

• Oh, thanks for telling me that. I'm here to show you a few new options that could help save you time and maybe money, which your current vendor is missing.

• Hey, you would be happy with me too if you gave me a chance. Please, please, please give me a chance.

• Maybe you think you're happy, but if I could see you this week, you will understand why many clients are switching to us. We are the best in this business. Don't you want to get service from the best too?

 "We are happy with our current vendor." If you'd like to have this client in the future, keep a tickler file and follow up at a later date. Try not to burn any bridges; keep the conversation light, and follow up often. Remember—not all clients are completely happy with their current vendors.

The good news is that most vendors eventually do something to disappoint their customers. Processes break down, and busy salespeople forget to follow up. Do not—and I mean do not—

trash the other vendor. This could backfire on you. For example, you never know if the vendor is the prospect's friend or family member. Win the business by creating and bringing value to the prospect.

5. "We just switched companies (or services)."

Say:

• How long ago was the switch? What was the main reason you selected this vendor? Can you share with me the area of responsibility they will take care of and your ROI expectation? We constantly enhance our business services, and I'd like to have the opportunity to bring you up to date on how we might be able to benefit you.

• Oh, I see. When did you switch? What was the reason for the switch? I am so sorry I wasn't able to provide a proposal for that. Are you under contract? For how long? Would you be interested in looking at one of our other services that your current vendor doesn't provide? I really would hate to lose you as a customer.

• Oh, I am sorry you did that. You may not know this but you made a very bad decision. That company has had a big problem with taking people's deposits and not delivering the product. I am sure you will be calling me back.

This is a perfect time to find out why they switched. What happened that caused the prospect to switch vendors? Use this information to remind future prospects that they will avoid these issues when buying from you. Also, remember —if prospects are the type you'd like to do business within the future, be sure to follow up with them every sixty to ninety days.

6. "Everyone is offering the same rate."

Say:

• This is a very competitive industry, and therefore it may seem that way. I would like to explain the differences between my company and my competitor's company and see if we can find a fit that works best for your needs. Does that seem agreeable to you?

• Thank you. I am curious ... when selecting a vendor, what else besides price is most important? Based on what you said, if I can satisfy those needs, can we meet to review how using us is possibly the best option?

• Thank you for letting me know. Not everyone can offer the same level of reliability, service, and support, so vendors can catch you off guard with price first. I'm curious how much you really know about their product quality and service?

• Everywhere I go, I think my competitors are following me around talking to my clients and offering them my prices. Well, you like me better, right? I mean, we've had a lot of lunches and ball games together. Honestly, you're my friend, right?

I love this "same rate" sales objection. The prospect is basically asking me to give a reason to go with my company. If the rate is the same, are the service, product, company, delivery, and technology the same? This is the perfect time to tell the prospect why your company is the best choice.

Another tip: start creating value before jumping to another discount. If you plan to discount the price, make sure you get a commitment from the prospect. Ask the prospect, "If I can get you a better value/price, will you do business with me?" If you don't get a commitment from the prospect before you make an adjustment, you may be cheating yourself out of a sale or a healthy profit margin. Why? Because the prospect will get you to make concessions and then call your competition and ask them the same thing. Be smart! Do not fall for this trap.

7. "We're moving."

Say:

• Really? That's wonderful! This is a good opportunity for you to make preparations to meet your product (or service) needs before you move. Once we review your needs, I can begin the process on my end to ensure that we meet your time re□uirements. The timing couldn't be better. Wouldn't you agree?

• Where are you moving to? Texas? Who would want to move there? That's just my opinion. Hmmm, I guess we won't be doing any more business, then. I don't service Texas.

When the prospect says, "We are moving," you want to sound excited about the move and ask where. When is the move date? What is the reason for the move? Are they growing? Are they consolidating locations?

You may find they are in the perfect position to need your products or services. Also pay attention to who may be moving into their space. This also could turn into a potential sale. Be helpful as well. You may not be able to service them, but you may know someone you could refer them to.

How will you know if they are bluffing? If they're truly moving, they will answer your questions. If it's a smoke screen, they will skirt, dodge, and avoid the issue. At least then you'll know they're bluffing, and you can move on to better opportunities.

8. "I'm too busy."

Say:

• I can respect that this isn't a convenient time. I honestly feel that if given fifteen minutes of your time, I can show you there is good synergy between our companies. My main goal is to show you how we can improve revenues and customer acquisition. I will be in your area next Thursday and Friday. Will either of those days work for you?

• Thank you. In light of your schedule, I understand how busy you are. Is there a better time? I've spent a lot of time reviewing your account, so we can review it □uickly and make appropriate changes based on your business re□uirements. Can I meet with you later today or tomorrow morning?

• Are you too busy to save your company money? Sounds lazy to me. I'm sure you would jump at the opportunity to save money on your personal budget, so why not your business' as well? What is two minutes of listening if it saves you twenty dollars a week? That's $960 a year. Besides, when you show the boss how much money you saved the company, there is more money available for your raise.

• Get over yourself. Everyone is busy! How am I supposed to help you if you tell me you're too busy? Slow down, take time to smell the roses, and meet with me so I can save you money. You do want to save money, don't you?

Don't be too pushy here. Believe them when they say, "I'm too busy." For prospects you want to do business with in the future, do the following:

• Be kind.

• Be sensitive.

• Ask if tomorrow would be better.

• Tell them you understand, and give them a good reason to see you at another time.

• Be consistent.

• Be diligent.

♣ Be kind … Did I say that already? Always be kind and polite. Gentle persistence always pays off.

9. "Your product is too complex."

Say:

• Many of my best clients thought that too. I can see that I may have confused you, or you may have some information that isn't correct. Can I take a few minutes to clarify how the product will support your business needs?

• What are you comparing our product to that makes you feel that way?

Don't Say:

• Plainly and simply, you won't know if something is too complex if you don't take the time to learn about it.

• I know – I think so too! I have to talk to one of our engineers to understand what the darn thing does, so I know how you feel. But the truth is that this product is just what the doctor ordered. Besides, if you buy this from me and I make □uota this month, I'll be eligible for the President's Club!

Listen closely to what prospects are telling you. Saying something is too complex is another way of telling you, "I don't see how your product fits into my business" or "I just don't understand all this technology language. I'm bored now, so please leave." Or they simply haven't had someone explain the product to them in a way they can understand.

Be sure you're speaking the right language to the right person. For instance, CEO-level people do not speak technology. They speak a language that deals with market share and market size. Tell them how your product or service can improve their market shares or sizes, and you have potential customers who will give you ten more minutes of their time.

Vice presidents and directors speak another language. They speak the language of improving business processes, coming in under budget, and increasing efficiency.

Managers and users speak the language of features and benefits. Since these people are closer to the actual performance line, they are the ones using the products' features and benefits.

If you speak the wrong language to any one of these people, they will be confused or bored out of their minds, which is a bad thing for you. In turn they may send a smoke signal to you: "Your product is too complex."

10. "Call me on Monday to set up an appointment."

Say:

• I have some time on Tuesday afternoon to meet with you. What time is best for you?

• How about we set up a tentative time for Tuesday, and I'll call to confirm on Monday?

• There's a promotion that ends soon, and I would like you to get the full savings and extra benefits before it expires. How about we meet either Tuesday or Wednesday of next week?

• Great! I'll call you on Monday. Let me get your e-mail address so I can send you confirmation for the appointment we set. I can see that you're busy and will call next Monday.

• I would be happy to call you back or to set up an appointment at a later time, but as a fellow business owner, I understand that calendars fill up □uickly. Why don't we set up a tentative appointment now? Would Tuesday two weeks from now or Thursday two weeks from now be better for you? Nine in the morning or three in the afternoon?

• Okay, well, I'm busy as well, but I'm not too busy to talk to you. So why don't we just schedule it now for next Monday and be done with it, since we're both busy people? I'm available at two. Can you make that time?

I like this objection because the prospect has opened the door to a possible meeting. When the prospect says, "Call me Monday," make a note on your calendar and call again on Monday. When you speak to customers, remind them of the re□uest that you call on Monday to schedule an appointment. This almost always ensures an appointment. Always be direct and up front about why you are calling. Avoid trying to sound like a long-lost friend. Prospects can tell when you're using a sales techni□ue to get the appointment. Just be honest, direct, to the point, persistent, and polite. Do this, and you will eventually have more appointments than you know what to do with.

11. "It's not a priority to us."

Say:

• Thank you for telling me that. Are you saying it's a priority later but just not right now?

• I understand it isn't a priority now. But I'm curious whether you can fit me in sometime next week to see if I can determine if there's a possible synergy between us. If I'm not able to, I'll be the first to tell you and be on my way. Just twenty minutes is all it will take.

• I understand that my product or service is not a priority for your business. However, if I could show you a solution to streamline the day-to-day operations of your business into a more efficient and cost-effective design, would that be a priority?

• Maybe you wouldn't be working so late if saving time were a priority.

• I have called you once a day for six weeks. Didn't your mama tell you it's rude not to return a phone call? Come on, give me a break!

When prospects throw this objection at you, stop and put yourself in their shoes. "It's not a priority" is another way of saying, "Your request isn't at the top of my list, but it is on the list somewhere." Your job is to help the client move this non-priority to a higher level. These counters from the field work well, so use them. Initiate questions quickly that get to the heart of the issue. When asking questions, remember to ask one and then wait for a response.

By the way, do you feel uncomfortable asking questions like "Are you telling me that employee loyalty to your organization is not a priority and that you don't have your employees' best interests in mind?" If this kind of question is difficult for you, consider getting out of the selling business. You may be more successful as an order taker.

Why? Because selling is about, well, selling! And initiating tough questions helps prospects follow you to a solution or helps you quickly qualify them as a low probability. To be successful at answering prospect objections you need to be able to ask hard questions.

12. "Just send me literature."

Say:

• If you would like me to send literature to you, does that mean you are somewhat interested? Who else would need to see a brochure?

• Sure, I will get some information out to you right away. Do you have an idea which product you would like to review? And when I send the literature, would you be interested in meeting with me to review it?

• I could send you general information; however, we customize our services to meet your needs in order to help you get the best results. If you have a few minutes, I could show you a few things on our website. Are you interested?

• I can send you literature, but it's usually best if I can meet with you as well. Is this something we can do?

• I would be happy to do that; however, may I first ask you a few ☐uestions so that the information I send will be pertinent to your needs?

• Oh sure, you bet. You want me to go ahead and put it in the trash can for you too?
Literature is expensive to print and mail, so don't send anything in the mail until you're sure there is a real interest. In many cases, the literature you send will be dumped in the trash. If you do mail literature to prospects, be sure to follow up in a week or two. I like to follow up with, "What did you like best about the literature I sent you?"

If they read it, they will have a good answer. If they didn't read it, they will feel embarrassed. Try to get a commitment from prospects to review the information within a few days. Even better, go over the literature on the phone or schedule an appointment.

Remember—if you can't get them back on the phone after you sent the literature, they most likely weren't interested in the first place. You just wasted the cost of the literature, envelope, postage, and your own time.

13. "Our corporate headquarters makes all the decisions."

Say:

• Great, thank you. Can you tell me who handles that on the local level?

• Although your company office makes the final decision, if you were to see something that could benefit your company, would you be able to make a recommendation?

• Could you give me the contact information for your corporate headquarters so I may present a proposal to them?

• Hey, man, I'm so sorry! I guess it's their loss.

• I guess you don't have any power at all. How does it feel to be low man on the totem pole?

Qualify early in cases where you may be dealing with a local office and decisions for your service or product are made elsewhere. The best strategy is to find someone who can champion your cause to the right people. That could be a gatekeeper or an end-user that prefers your service or information they could provide. Get information that will help you get to the right person.

Once you find the right person, start a prospecting strategy that will get you noticed. Be careful that you aren't wasting time and money on an opportunity that will go nowhere. Qualify the prospect to be sure this is a good business fit for you too. Not all opportunities are your opportunities.

14. "I need guaranteed results."

Say:

• Perfect, that's why I'm here. I would expect the same. My company offers a full money-back guarantee if we don't meet your expectations.

• I completely agree. There is no risk on your part. None whatsoever. Is this your only reason not to move forward?

• No problem! All successful clients feel the same way. I can understand your need for proven results. Has there been a problem with unmet expectations in the past?

• I can guarantee the results as long as you agree to do the things we discuss.

• If you need a guarantee, buy an insurance policy! I mean, I don't have control of everything.

Prospects use this objection for several reasons:

• They don't want to look bad to their boss.

• They've been burned in the past.

• They want an escape clause just in case.

• They want the security of knowing you believe in your own product.

Prospects that use this objection need you to be a partner, so be sure to use words like we and us . This will feel more collaborative. Make your prospects feel safe by explaining how the warranty or guarantee will benefit them. Buyers don't want to feel trapped if your product or service doesn't meet their expectations. So offering "money back" or "cancellation in thirty days" will help you close deals faster.

15. "I tried your product before, and it didn't work."

Say:

• I'm sorry. What happened? How did you use it? What was the result? What could have been done better?

• I know how you feel. Let me ask you, have you ever had a meal at a restaurant that didn't meet your expectations? Does that mean you would never eat at the restaurant again? Maybe your last experience with this product was like that. Could we start over?

• I'm very sorry and understand your frustration. We have several clients in your industry that use this product (or service) without any issues. Do you think it would be okay to revisit it and see how we can improve things?

Don't Say:

• When did you use my product? Everyone loves it! Are you sure you were using it correctly? A lot of people your age just need more training.

This is a common objection when someone has used your product before and didn't have a very good experience. I bought a car once that was a complete lemon; however, the manufacturer has made improvements over the years, and today the same company is a leading car producer.

The point is, when prospects have had a bad experience, get them to share with you what went wrong. Don't argue with them about their experience, because you will be fighting a losing battle. Empathize with your prospects and focus on what happened. Show you care by listening to what made their experiences less than perfect.

16. "How can you service multiple accounts? I don't want to get lost."

Say:

• Your company is very important to us, and that's why we have an assigned team of specialists to manage your specific needs. There are approximately four members assigned to your account, so you can see the ratio is quite good. And these resources are available to us both, so that I can manage your accounts.

• Oh, don't you worry about it. You can trust me!

Your prospects are looking for security, and security is what you need to give them. Many customers want "service after the sale," meaning they bought a product or service trusting they were going to get an acceptable level of service after the purchase. Poor service experiences lead a prospect to question how you can service so many accounts. It's not an objection that comes up often. However, if this question is asked and you are indifferent about it, you could possibly tip the scales away from you and toward your competition.

17. The decision maker won't return your calls.

Say:

• (To the gatekeeper) Hi, my name is Stepp Sydnor. Can you help me? I am trying to get a meeting with Mr. Diehard and seem to be having a difficult time getting an appointment. Is there a better way to do this? What's your advice?

• (On voice mail) Hi, Mr. Diehard, I know how busy you are. In our last meeting, you asked me to get back with you today. When you get a free minute, please call me on my cell phone. That number is 818-888-9988. Thank you, I will try you again later.

• (To a gatekeeper) Hey, cutie, your boss and I have been playing phone tag. He is insistent that I get in touch with him so how about you be a good receptionist and get him on the phone for me?

• (On voicemail) You must be ignoring my phone calls. I have left several messages for you with no response. You have until close of business Friday to take advantage of the low cost deal we discussed. If I don't hear from you, it's your loss man.

The decision maker won't take your calls. Do you actually expect decision makers to drop everything they're doing and call you? If so, you need to get out of this business. This is why we call it "sales." You need to get creative and stay determined as well as stay polite and kind. Too aggressive and you're toast. Too soft and you'll give up too early.

If you are prospecting and trying to get the decision maker to see you, try something different. One time I sent the general manager of a radio station an old cowboy boot filled with goodies (candy, a gift card to a coffee shop, playing cards, etc.) With a note that said, "Howdy. I've determined I have something to help you improve your sales. I have traveled a long way to see you. Can we meet? If so, I will bring the other boot."

Decision makers are busy. So be consistent and tenacious. People respect your diligence. Also, never expect that they will call you back. If you have this expectation, you will only disappoint yourself. If you keep calling once a week for seven weeks, eventually someone will reach out to you and say:

• Stop calling (usually an assistant).

• Yes, sorry i've been busy, but let's meet soon (so you will stop calling).

• Yes, let's meet. Are there any more salespeople like you? Because I need some on my team.

18. "Why do you want copies of my bills?"

Say:

• People have often told me how confusing their bills are. One of the objectives for our meeting is to help clarify what you are paying for and see if we can change anything to improve the service and possibly reduce the cost. Does that sound like something that can help you?

• This is so I can make sure we aren't missing something. I also want to identify exactly what you're getting from your current vendor.

• Wow, I really struck a nerve with you. Are you hiding something? Hey, I just asked to see your records so I can show you how much you may be getting ripped off. Gee, sorry I asked.

As a salesperson, in many industries, you will often want to see a customer's past billing records so you can present a sales proposal that includes or exceeds the products or services they are currently receiving. Customers can become suspicious because they don't understand your true motive. Let them know what your motive is, and most prospects will hand over the goods. If they feel you're pulling a sales trick, they'll throw up a wall of rejection.

If they object to giving you their bill(s), just assume they're concerned about you seeing what they're paying. Let your prospects know that they can mark out the pricing if that's their concern. In many situations, the buyer will find it a hassle marking out the price and will just deliver the bill(s) to you.

19. "Let me check with my partner/husband/wife."

Say:

I understand! I will note on the contract that it is subject to his (or her) approval. May I note on your account that you've okayed that? Once we get the second okay, we'll be ready to proceed.

I'm curious if this is something you want to do. Is this a product or service that will help you ? If so, can we meet with your partner now?

If you feel that this is a good idea for your business, will your partner say yes as well?

When do you plan to meet with your partner? Can I call you this afternoon and confirm the start date?

What questions will he (or she) have? Let's talk about them now.

When will it be convenient for us to get together again? I'd like him (or her) to be there as well.

Don't say:

Really? You aren't important enough to pull the trigger?

I hate being tied down and made to feel like I can't think for myself. Can't you just make a good decision and tell your partner how it's going to be?
Hey, it's more fun to ask for forgiveness than permission, right?

"Let me check with my partner/husband/wife." Prequalify before the meeting what the decision-making process is and confirm who will be present for the meeting. For sales where a spouse is usually involved, prequalification is especially necessary.

20. "The economy and slow business are hurting our company."

Say :

• Then I'm glad I came to see you today! I have some specific plans that will help increase business. I can show you how to move more products despite the economy.

• What are you currently doing to improve your situation? Let me show you what we're doing to help other companies like yours improve business.

• I understand. I can show you how, in many economic slowdowns, the companies that rethink how they're going to market always do better. Let me show you what we're doing to help companies like yours.

• Thanks, that's why I'm here. People are still buying, and they should be buying from you. Let's take a look at what you're currently doing and see how we can meet your customers' needs with my products.

• Do you think you're reacting to the notion that nobody is buying? People still have money to spend; let's make sure they know to come to you.

Don't Say:

Why the heck are you in business? Whining and complaining isn't going to help. Put your big-kid pants on and deal with it.

"The economy and slow business are hurting our company." When hard economic times hit businesses, owners are generally uncertain and stall on new ideas or services. Be sure to have success stories you can share about individuals who, despite economic downturns, have done well. For example, did you know that Microsoft and Hewlett Packard started in a depressed economy?

21. "My budget is already spent."

Say:

• If we put the budget aside for a moment, how much would the company need to get back as a return on the investment to justify the cost?

• Do you mean the budget is already spent, or do you mean it is already allocated?

• In our last conversation, you said you had control over your department's budget. Do you believe the program (or product) will bring you more business? If not, why? If so, can we move or adjust the budget?

• If you had the budget, would you do the program?

Don't Say:

It takes money to make money! Can you print a copy of your budget and let me analyze it?

Hey, there are two kinds of people in the world: winners and losers! If you want to be a winner, you're going to have to take a risk.

"My budget is already spent." When buyers use this objection, it can mean one of two things:

• They really don't have the money.

• They don't want to put the money into your product or solution.

In either case, ask the buyer questions about the business. This will give you an idea where the value is. Buyers buy because your solution solves a business problem. If you don't ask questions about the business—such as "Who is your competition and how are you positioning the company to grow more market share?"—you won't know how to work yourself into their budgets.

22. "Your rates are too high."

Say:

• I understand. That's why I'm here! Can you tell me why you feel the rate is too high?

• I agree that other providers' prices are lower than mine, but our price is our price. Is there a reason you haven't already placed this order with them? Let's talk about the differences in our services.

• We service 55 percent of the market in your area. And most companies tell us our price value is lower than that of other vendors. Can you give me an idea why you feel our rates are too high?

• You're saying the price is too high, right? Then which part of my proposal do you feel you can work without?

Don't say:

You know, it's your loss if you don't take this deal. Other vendors are less expensive because their service is horrible. I'm pretty sure I heard a rumor that your current provider is going out of business anyway.

Why do you think people prefer quality over price? Any smart person can see that we are number one in the marketplace.

"Your rates are too high." In a highly competitive market, this is a common objection. The knee-jerk reaction is to discount the service. Don't do this. Instead, create value. Clients will pay for value. Another idea is to put their current business goals at risk by helping them to see what happens if they don't buy your product.

23. "Business is good. Why do I need this?"

Say:

• Thanks for asking me that. That's why I'm here. We have a track record of improving business results a minimum of 20 percent, even when business is good. If you have a few minutes, we can discuss your current situation, and I can tell you more about what we are doing and see if it makes sense to do business together.

• Great! I'll let people know that so they won't be coming in here offering you anything since business is SO good.

• I hear you! Business is good for maybe you. But it could be better right?
"Business is good. Why do I need this?" When a prospect's business is doing well, they typically won't be interested in

changing what is currently working for them. You need to get the focus off the status quo and direct the conversation in your favor with these questions:

• When business was not doing good what was the reason?

• Now that business is doing good can you share with me what you're doing different?

• How is your competition doing? And how are they insuring their future success?

• What is the benefit to the business future if there was a solution to sustain business success? Would you be open to a discussion around this solution?

24. "I can't afford it."

Say:

• Perfect, I'm glad you said that. Many of my current clients had the same concern in the beginning. Are you saying that if you could afford it, this is something you would seriously consider?

• I understand you can't afford it, and I don't want you to go over budget. Is this service or product something you would do if you had the money? Yes? Then I have some terms that will fit your budget.

• If you work with a plan we create together, we can generate revenue for your company five times what you're spending on the product. Here's a success story from one of our other clients.

• Well, the good news is that it sounds like you're interested in our product (or service); is that safe to say?

• Come on, you can do better than that ole standby objection. Are you a business college graduate? Sounds like you need help from a financial business consultant to get your finances in order.

"I can't afford it."

Be sure in the first meeting or discussion that you test the client's ability to purchase. Qualify your clients by asking them if they have purchased a service like this in the past. What did they spend? What was their experience? Be sure to give them a high and low dollar number to prepare them for the investment so that it isn't a shock.

I like to say, "Have you used outside consultants in the past? Are you familiar with fees charged by training companies? Based on what you told me, an initial proposal would be $5,000 on the low end and $15,000 on the high end. Is this what you were expecting?" If they fall out of their chair and grab their chest, you know they don't have the money for your product and you are wasting your time.

25. "You are the third rep who has called me in six months."

Say:

• Well, that is why I'm calling now. I can see how frustrating this must be for you. We are just so excited about this opportunity that we've all been trying to show as many people we can about it. Can I ask you a few questions? Would you have time to meet and give me your opinion about this opportunity?

• I understand. We have a lot of marketing initiatives going on. If I were you, I would feel the same way. Establishing a relationship takes time. That's what I'm here to do with you.

• Each Quarter our company identifies key companies that are positioned for growth. It looks like your company has been selected more than once. I'm sorry about the duplication. I know that's frustrating. While I'm here, can I ask you a few Questions? How is your company positioned for growth in the next three to six months?

Don't Say:

Is this a problem for you? People do change jobs, you know. Just be happy our company wants to do business with you.

You seem kind of sensitive about this. I mean, geez, give me a break.

"You are the third rep who has called me in six months." Imagine you have a small business and in one month four different account representatives from the same company drop by. As a salesperson, you're going to get some misplaced aggression from the prospect. Your first response is to empathize.

Beware of "I'm sorry" statements. Don't apologize; empathize. Say you "understand," and tell them why you understand, such as "I know this is frustrating. I would feel the same way if I were bombarded with too many sales calls from the same company."

26. "The home office won't let me."

Say:

• Thank you for letting me know that. I have one question: Can you direct me to the person I should speak with at the home office?

• I appreciate the information. Can you advise me what I should do to get an audience with the right people at the home office?

• If you could make the decision, is this a service or product you would choose? Why or why not?

Don't Say:

• There is an exception to every rule. How do we break the rules and think outside the box?

• There are leaders and there are followers. Which are you?

• Let's call them right now and let me do all the talking.

"The home office won't let me." This objection is either true or false. Ask this question to discover if what they are saying is a reality or just a stall: "What is the process your company goes through to make a purchase like this?"
This question will help you understand what's behind the objection.

27. "Call me next month."

Say:

• I will be happy to follow up with you in a month. I have one question: Can I send you a calendar invite through my e-mail system with a date in mind?

• It seems I haven't done a very good job explaining why we should meet and why next month could be too late for you to take advantage of the specials I have to offer.

• You're not saying that to get me to leave, are you? Just take a minute to look at my plan.

• You're busy and so am I. Let's set up a time right now and stop dillydallying around. Time is money!

"Call me next month." This is a very common response. A reason they may not want to meet now is because they don't see a good enough reason to meet with you at all. Be sure to highlight the business benefits other companies are getting from your solution. The best techni☐ue is to use a verbal success story. Verbal success stories get people's attention; however, they have to be crafted and rehearsed for maximum effect. They cannot be more than two to three minutes long. This is the structure I use, and it's effective:

• What is the problem?

• What is the solution (make it brief)?

• What are the measurable results (from your current clients)?

28. "I don't like your manager."

Say:

• Thanks for telling me that. That's why I'm here. What was it that caused you not to like the manager?

• Can you explain to me what happened? Is this something I can help resolve?

Don't say:

• I respect your opinion. But the real conversation we should be having is what I can do to help you grow your business.

• Now wait a minute. Do you like every item on a restaurant's menu? I don't think so. You still eat there, right? Well, I am a different person on the menu. Let's talk business!

• Quite frankly, I think the manager is an idiot. We're on the same page with that one.

"I don't like your manager." This is a perfect example of an objection that sometimes causes salespeople to undermine their company and look completely unprofessional. You should never throw your coworker under the bus. This always backfires and makes you look untrustworthy.

And it doesn't solve anything. Coworkers will drop the ball, but tomorrow you may drop the ball. And some coworkers have poor relationship skills and say or do things that don't sit well with buyers. In any case, never, never, never bad-mouth your company or a coworker.

What you want to do is stop selling your idea and start listening to the story behind this objection. The fact that you're interested will cause buyers to open up. If they don't want to open up, don't push the issue. Just follow up in a few weeks and try to get into a conversation about how valuable your product or service is despite their opinion of your manager.

29. "E-mail it to me. I'll call you when I'm ready."

Say:

• You're telling me to send you my literature and I'd love to do that. I'd also like a guarantee you're going to look it over so let's set an appointment for next week to discuss any ⬜uestions you may have.

• I'd be happy to e-mail you. Our packet contains a lot of information, and I don't want to overload you. Do you mind if I ask you just a couple of quick questions so I can send only the specific information that you'd be most interested in?"

• Are you kidding me? You probably won't even read my e-mail. I think you're just blowing me off, so I don't really want to send you anything! Let's just talk about it now.

"E-mail it to me. I'll call you when I'm ready." How do you handle this type of stall? I suggest you call their bluff. Many salespeople simply take this "e-mail it to me" objection and comply with the request. It's okay to comply with prospects, but do it on your terms. Test the waters with the counters above. If they don't give you an answer, you can do the following:

Send just enough information to get them interested in knowing more.

Send a letter with your contact information attached.

If the prospects are genuine in their response, they won't mind answering your questions. So test the waters before you send loads of material that will most likely overload them and get overlooked.

30. "Your company messed things up last time."

Say:

• I'm so sorry! That's why I'm here. Can you tell me what happened?

• Can you tell me what went wrong? Once I know the full story, let me see if I can make things right.

• That's why I have an installation checklist. We've changed some of our processes based on feedback from our clients. This checklist, along with key contact numbers, will keep you informed so we don't drop the ball.

• You know your company isn't perfect. We aren't perfect either. So give me a break and let me earn your business.

How do you handle these situations when they come up in your business? You drop the ball too, so lighten up a little.

"Your company messed things up last time." When your company drops the ball on buyers, the worst thing you can do is ignore what they have to say about it. I have seen many salespeople completely ignore what a buyer is trying to tell them. The best response is to acknowledge the statement and ask for clarification.

Listening to people doesn't mean you're waiting for your turn to talk. Blowing by an objection like this will confirm that you aren't the company to do business with. Slow down and find out what happened. You don't have to agree with what they said. You only need to listen and put yourself in their shoes by using effective empathy statements.

If you were the buyer and this happened to you, wouldn't you react the same way? Listening and repeating back to prospects what they say lowers their frustration and brings your relationship to a neutral position. You can always go up from there. Trying to give buyers instructions when they have issues with your company opens up the possibility of hostility toward you.

31. "I told my friends I'd use their company."

Say:

• Thanks for letting me know. Can you explain what problem this solution will solve? Do you think their company will be able to handle all phases of this process?

• That's great. We can let them handle the major project. Would you like to see if there is something specific I can help you with that may work with your friend's services or benefit you as well as their plan?

Don't say:

You know what happens with a friend deal, don't you? Playing family politics can get you fired. Do you really want to risk your job?

"I told my friends I'd use their company." This objection is a common one. The goal isn't to boot the competition out. That would end up working against you. Don't challenge prospects' decisions either. Instead, praise them for their choice. Thank them for letting you know.

Then ask questions that will uncover other business problems you may be able to solve. You may not be able to do anything for them at this time, but stay in touch and see how the project is coming along. Down the road, if there is a failure in service or product, the buyer will be glad you stayed in touch. The friendly relationship could eventually turn sour, and you want to be first in line to pick up the ball if that happens.

32. "Is this the best price I can get?"

Say:

• Yes, this is the best price you can get! (Pause and wait for a response.)
I can give you a better price, but we'll need to see what options you want to exclude from the package.

• I already discounted the price for this product (or service) up front because you mentioned, in our last conversation, about the budget that you can't exceed. Here is the amount of discount I applied.

Don't say:

Sure, take another 20 percent off. I knew you were going to say something like this.

You're driving a $100,000 car. I think you can afford this price.

"Is this the best price I can get?" This is one of the most common price objections. The best response is to tell them yes, this is the best price. Then wait for their response. In many cases, prospects are going to buy from you either way. Pause after the ⬚uestion and see what happens. If their second response is another objection, you know there's an opportunity to negotiate the deal until both parties have a win-win outcome.

33. "It's too expensive."

Do say:

• "I'd love to unpack [product's] features and how it can help with the issue of [prospect problem] you shared with me."

Price objections are the most common type of objection and are even voiced by prospects who have every intention of buying. Beware — the moment you start focusing on price as a selling point, you reduce yourself to a transactional middleman. Instead, circle back to the product's value.

34. "There's no money."

Do say:

"I understand. Allow me to explain our other offerings that may be a better fit for your current growth levels and budget."

It could be that your prospect's business simply isn't big enough or generating enough cash right now to afford a product like yours. Track their growth and see how you can help your prospect get to a place where your offering would fit into their business.

35. "We don't have any budget left this year."

Do say:

• "Let's schedule a follow-up call for when you expect funding to return. When do you think that may be?"

A variation of the "no money" objection, what your prospect's telling you here is that they're having cash flow issues. But if there's a pressing problem, it needs to get solved eventually. Either help your prospect secure budget from executives to buy now, or arrange up a follow-up call for when they expect funding to return.

36. "We need to use that budget somewhere else."

Do say:

• "We had a customer with a similar issue, but by purchasing [product] they were actually able to increase their ROI and assign some of their new revenue to other parts of the budget."

Prospects sometimes try to earmark resources for other uses. It's your job to make your product/service a priority that deserves budget allocation now. Share case studies of similar companies that have saved money, increased efficiency, or had a massive ROI with you.

37. "I don't want to get stuck in a contract."

Do say:

• "I understand. Let's talk about some different contract terms and payment schedules that I can offer you. Perhaps these would be a better fit."

A prospect with a genuine need and interest who balks at time-based contract terms is generally hesitant for cash flow reasons. Luckily for you, there are workarounds — find out if you can offer month-by-month or ⬚uarter-by-⬚uarter payment instead of asking for a year or more commitment upfront.

38. "We're already working with [Vendor A]."

Do say:

• "Why did you choose [vendor]? What's working well? What's not? Allow me to explain how [product] is different."

Common sales objections and rebuttals about the competition. A prospect who's working with a competitor is a blessing in disguise. They've already recognized a need and identified a solution; much of the education you'd otherwise be responsible for has already been done. You can spend your time doing the one thing you'd have to hold off on with a prospect who hasn't recognized their pain yet — talk about your product.

Just because a prospect is working with a competitor doesn't mean they're happy with them. Probe into the relationship and pay special attention to complaints that could be solved with your product.

39. "I'm locked into a contract with a competitor."

Do say:

• "How is your relationship with [competitor]? Perhaps I can offer a discount to make up for the cost of switching over to work with us."

Perhaps the easiest competitor-related objection to handle, this phrase is worded in a way that broadcasts your prospect's feeling of being trapped. See if you can come up with a creative discount to offset the cost of breaking a contract early, or demonstrate ROI that will make up for the sunk cost.

Of course, your prospect could have simply chosen an overly negative turn of phrase. Ask questions about their relationship with the competitor to determine whether they're actually happy or are itching for a vendor switch.

40. "I can get a cheaper version of your product somewhere else."

Do say:

• "What are the points of differentiation between [product] and your other option? What provides you with the most value and support?

Find out what you're dealing with here. Are you in a competitive situation, and the prospect is playing you against a competitor to drive up discounts? Or is your prospect under the impression that a similar, cheaper product can do everything they need?

If it's the former, lay out your deepest discount and emphasize the features that make your product superior. Walk away if they ask you to go lower. In the second scenario, take advantage of the comparison. Play the differences up and emphasize overall worth, not cost.

41. "I'm happy with [Competitor X]."

Do say:

• "That's great. What components of the product or relationship are you most satisfied with? I'd love to learn more and see how we may compare."

What if your prospect is happy? The same strategy still applies — find out why they believe their relationship with your competitor is beneficial, and identify weak spots where your product could do better.

42. "Competitor X says [false statement about your product]."

Do say:

• "We manufacture our products in Canada, not Thailand. I have a map of our factories and distribution routes if you'd like to see it."

According to the creator of Your Sales MBA Jeff Hoffman, salespeople should first respond with, "That's not true," then pause.

Hoffman says 90% of the time this reply will satisfy the buyer and they'll move on. You'll seem confident and collected, whereas your competitor will seem desperate and insecure.

If your prospect is still unsure, they'll ask another ⬚uestion. At that point, you can provide more background in your rebuttal.

43. "I'm not authorized to sign off on this purchase."

Do say:

• "Who is the right person to speak to regarding this purchase? Can you redirect me to them, please?"

This is a common sales objections and rebuttals about authorization, No problem. Ask your prospect the name of the right person to speak to, and then redirect your call to them.

44. "I can't sell this internally."

Do say:

• "What objections do you think you'll face? Can I help you prepare the business case for when you speak with your decision-makers? I may have some enablement materials I can share to help."

Well, your prospect might not be able to, but you can. After all, you sell your product every day. Ask your prospect what objections they anticipate, and help them prepare the business case for adopting your product. Check with Marketing to see if there's any collateral you can leverage on your prospect's behalf.

45. "[Economic buyer] isn't convinced."

Do say:

• "That's too bad. If anything changes, please don't hesitate to contact me. I'd love to help you get your team onboard."

If you've already addressed objection #12 by providing internal selling advice and coaching and your prospect just can't hack it, it might be time to walk away. While it's heart-rending to give up on a prospect who's on your side and just can't convince the higher-ups, it's also a waste of your time to keep butting heads with someone who will never see your product's value.

46. "We're being downsized / bought out."

Do say:

• Thank you for your time and for speaking with me regarding this product. If you're ever in need of [product or service], please don't hesitate to contact me."

This happens rarely, but when it does, there's usually nothing you can do. If there's no more company, there's no more deal. Wrap the relationship professionally so when your prospect finds a new gig, they'll be more likely to restart the conversation from a new company.

47. "There's too much going on right now."

Do say:

• "I understand. What are some of your competing priorities? I'd love to schedule a follow-up call for when your calendar clears up."
Ask your prospect to define their competing priorities for you. If they can't, it's likely a brush-off and you should press them on precisely why they don't want to engage with you.

If they can provide concrete answers, don't sweat it. Set a meeting time for a follow-up and send over helpful resources in the meantime to stay on your prospect's radar.

48. "I'm part of a buying group."

Do say:

• "Are there limits on whom you can buy from? What price are you currently receiving? What companies belong to your buying coalition?"

Buying groups enable independent companies to team up and make joint purchases from vendors — usually getting a far better price than they'd be able to secure on their own.

If your company isn't on their list of approved suppliers, however, your prospect probably won't be interested. After all, you can't offer them the same discount for purchasing in bulk.

Respond to this objection by delving into the details of their membership. When you've learned more, you can decide whether it makes economic sense for this prospect to work with you — and if there's an opportunity to become one of their buying group's vendors.

49. "I've never heard of your company."

Do say:

• "We're a company that sells ad space on behalf of publishers like yourself. I'd love to speak with you about your revenue model and see if we can help."

Common sales objections and rebuttals about not having heard of the companytreat this objection as a re□uest for information. Don't give an elevator pitch, but provide a very □uick summary of your value proposition.

50. "We're doing great in X area."

If you hear this objection, ask a few more clarifying □uestions and do a little more □ualification.

Do say:

• "What are your goals? How much progress has been made?"

51. "We don't have that business pain."

Do say:

• "Interesting. What solutions are you currently using to address that area of your business?

This objection is often raised as a brush-off, or because prospects haven't realized they're experiencing a certain problem yet. And while ultimately you might discover they really don't need your product, don't take this objection at face value.

52. "X problem isn't important right now."

Do say:

• "Tell me more about that. What are your current priorities?"

Sometimes, a simple "Oh?" will be enough for your prospect to start talking. Listen closely for real reasons the need has low priority versus platitudes. Keep in mind that excuses can be a sign that your prospect understands they have a problem and is trying to rationalize their inaction. Capitalize on this and instill a sense of urgency.

53. "I don't see what your product could do for me."

Do say:

• "Interesting. Can you share what specific challenges you're facing right now? Perhaps [product] presents a solution we have yet to discuss."

Another re☐uest for information packaged as an objection. Reconfirm the goals or challenges you've discussed and explain how your product can solve specific problems.

54. "I don't understand your product."

Do say:

• "What aspects of the product are confusing to you? I'd love to connect you to a customer success technician or product engineer to help you better understand how we can help you."

If your prospect literally can't wrap their head around your product, that's a bad sign. If your product is particularly complicated or specialized, it may be time to disqualify your prospect lest they churn two months from now.

Don't give up immediately, though. Ask your prospect what aspects of your product they're unclear on, then try explaining it in a different way. Alternatively, bring in a technician or product engineer to answer questions out of your depth.

55. "I've heard complaints about you from [company]."

Do say:

• "Thanks for sharing that feedback with me. I'll pass it along to [relevant department]. While we're on the phone, would you be interested in hearing a few tips for improving your average invoicing turnaround time?"

Word-of-mouth reviews are powerful, which can be both a blessing and a curse. Rather than immediately defending your solution, business, or brand — which will only validate the criticism — thank them for sharing the feedback with you. Then follow up with an offer to add value.

This gives you an opportunity to establish credibility and trust with your prospect. Once you've given them a positive experience, they'll naturally form a high opinion of you.

56. "We don't have capacity to implement the product."

Do say:

• "I hear you, and I want [product] to add value, not take it away. What are your current day-to-day responsibilities in your job? I'd love to explain how the product, once onboarded, can alleviate some of those."

This objection can be a deal-killing roadblock. Depending on what product you sell, it's possible your prospect will have to add headcount or divert resources to fully take advantage of your offering, and if they truly aren't able to, you might have to dis ualify them.

Another tactic is to assess your prospect's current duties and day-to-day to see what job responsibilities could potentially be eliminated or made easier by your product.

57. "Your product is too complicated."

Do say:

• "What features are confusing to you? Remember, our customer service team will be available 'round-the-clock to help with implementation."

Common sales objections and rebuttals about the product being complicatedfind out if your prospect is confused about specific features or if the product is indeed over their head. If it's the latter, you might have to disqualify.

But if it's the former, remind your prospect that they'll have help from your customer service team should they choose to buy and that you'll be on hand to answer any implementation questions they have.

58. "You don't understand my challenges. I need help with Y, not X."

Do say:

• "I apologize! Allow me to restate my understanding of your challenges, and please let me know what I'm missing or misstating."

It's crucial to make your prospect feel heard. Restate your impression of their situation, then align with your prospect's take and move forward from there. A lot of misunderstandings and hard feelings can be resolved simply by rephrasing your prospect's words.

59. "You don't understand my business."

Do say:

• "Sorry — I assumed X was true, but it looks like that doesn't apply to your business. Can you tell me a little more about X?"

If you sell to a specific industry, chances are you do know a bit about your prospect's business. Let them know that you have experience working with similar companies, and have solved similar problems in the past.

If you simply made an incorrect assumption about your prospect's company or industry, don't be afraid to own up to it. Your prospects will appreciate your candor.

60. "Your product doesn't have X feature, and we need it."

Do say:

• "Have you checked out [partner or conjoining product]? It's a good fit with ours and can be used alongside it to solve for Y."

Try suggesting a supplementary product that can be used in conjunction with yours. But if that specific need is a must-have and your product can't solve it, your prospect might not be a good fit. Time to disqualify and move along to a better-fit opportunity.

61. "We're happy the way things are."

Do say:

• "That's great! Can you tell me how you're currently solving for X?"
Maybe everything really is going swimmingly. But more likely, your prospect is having some sort of challenge (after all, who isn't?).

Do some light qualification to determine if they're facing any problems you can solve, then move forward or disqualify based on their answers.

62. "I don't see the potential for ROI."

Do say:

• "I'd love to show you. Can we schedule a time for me to explain our product's potential to deliver a high ROI to you and your team?"

This is a sign that you'll have to prepare a formal pitch for either your contact or their managers, either using internal numbers provided by your prospect or customer case studies. Nothing sells quite like hard numbers.

63. "X is just a fad."

Do say:

• "I understand why you may think that! Let's schedule a time for me to walk through how our product helped some other businesses like yours find success with X — and why it's here to stay."

You might hear this objection if your product pioneers a concept that's new to your prospect's industry. For example, social media is now widely accepted as a necessary part of a sound business strategy, but seven years ago many would have scoffed at it.

Now is the time to pull out any testimonials or customer case studies you have to prove ROI of your product. If you're pioneering a new concept or practice, you'll have to show that it works.

64. "Your product doesn't work with our current [tools, set-up]."

Do say:

• "Which tools are you currently using? How integral are those tools to your [strategy]? What do those products help you accomplish?"

Common sales objections and rebuttals about integration with current tools. This objection can be a deal-breaker if the buyer is committed to their existing solutions. However, sometimes your product will replace these tools or make them obsolete. A workaround may be possible as well.

To find out, ask some ⬜uestions.

65. "Your product sounds great, but I'm too swamped right now to handle [implementation, roll-out]."

Do say:

• "I understand. It typically takes our customers [X days/weeks] to get fully up and running with [product]. How many minutes a day do you spend on [task]?"
Prospects are often put off by the effort re□uired to switch products, even if the ROI is substantial.

To empathize with them, prove that you're trustworthy, and ensure they do have the bandwidth. Next, combat their reluctance to change by digging into the costs or pains of their current situation.

Calculate what they stand to gain — in time, efficiency, money, or all of the above.

66. "*Click.*"

Do say:

• "Sorry, looks like we got disconnected! Do you have a few minutes?"
If your prospect hangs up on you, don't sweat it — it happens to everyone eventually. Try reaching out to a different person at the company using a different approach.

Or you can go on the offensive. Wait a few seconds, then call back. Which approach you choose is purely dependent on how your conversation with your prospect went before the hang-up.

67. "I'm busy right now."

Of course your prospect is busy — almost every professional is these days. Simply explain that you're not looking to give a full-blown conversation, just have a □uick chat about whether or not a longer discussion about your product would be a good fit at their organization.

Do say:

• "I don't want to take up too much of your time. Can we have a ꓳuick chat about your challenges with X and how [product] may help?"

68. "I'm not interested."

Do say:

• "I understand. Can we schedule a time for a follow-up call? In the meantime, I can send over some resources so you can learn more."

During a prospecting call, it's far too early for a prospect to be able to definitively say they are or aren't interested in your product. Offer to send over some resources and schedule a follow-up call.

69. "Call me back next quarter."

Do say:

• "I'll touch base next quarter. Before we hang up, I'd love to get a sense of how your next quarter will go. Do you feel you'll get the go-ahead from your superiors?"

Prospects will often say this to dissuade you from pursuing a conversation. But don't let them off that easily — it's a vague brush-off uttered in the hopes you'll fade away and disappear. Ask some ꓳuestions to find out their motivations for brushing you off.

70. "How did you get my information?"

Do say:

• "I came across your website in my research and believe that [product] would be a great fit for you."

Hopefully, you're not pulling numbers from lists you got off the internet — because if you are, your prospects have every reason to be annoyed. Don't get defensive — simply remind the prospect that they filled out a form on your site, or signed up for more information at a trade show, or that you simply came across their website and wanted to reach out to see if you could help.

Final Thoughts

In this book, I prepared the top 70 objections I got throughout my career in Sales, working in the tech industry in different sectors. You might wonder, why certain objection you were expecting didn't came up on the list, or didn't made it to the cut: I tried to avoid duplicate content, as, for example, if someone asks you to call back next month, quarter or year, you can use the same handling, so, instead of creating ten more for each timeframe (day, month, week, quarter, lunar year, etc).

The pages you went through, are meant to be a guide and a handbook, something that is easilly available at your desk, and ideally should be consulted continuously. This series is also designed do demistify and create more structure on this complicated, complex and rewarding sales environment, so if you haven't already, check out my page www.fcbohnke.com for more books on sales and surrounding topics.

I hope you enjoyed this book, best of luck in handling your objections, and don't forget: no master fell from the sky – it's all about practice, practice and practice. Test it out, follow this method, and as soon as you get more experience in the field, try, twist and adapt it according to what works for YOU.